P9-BIX-234

DECADENCE

RICHARD GILMAN

DECADENCE

The Strange Life
of an Epithet

Farrar, Straus and Giroux
New York

Portions of this book appeared, in somewhat different form,
in *American Review* 22 and *Partisan Review*

Library of Congress Cataloging in Publication Data
Gilman, Richard.
Decadence: the strange life of an epithet.
1. Decadence (The English word) I. Title.
PE1599.D43G54   1979   422   78–32039

For Richard Poirier

DECADENCE

1

Words TAKE ON LIFE FROM A PARTICULAR environment and time, but certain of them live on beyond their proper course and duration. Most archaic words have obeyed inexorable linguistic laws; the life has gone out of them and they remain merely as historical artifacts, coinage from an earlier realm of the mind. But there are words that are not so docile, so tractable. They hang on, simulating existence, lending themselves for use with an alacrity that ought to make us suspicious. Certain words of a moral or behavioral kind, judgmental words, continue to insinuate themselves into contexts where they injure meaning and bring about confusion, since they carry with them a *previousness,* something once true, something, that is to say, once applicable. There are words in use now that are no longer applicable.

"I like the word 'decadent,'" Paul Verlaine wrote nearly a century ago. "All shimmering with purple and gold . . . it throws out the brilliance of flames and the gleam of precious stones. It is made up of carnal spirit and unhappy flesh and of all the violent splendors of the Lower Empire; it conjures up the paint of the courtesans, the sports of the circus, the breath of the tamers of animals, the bounding of wild beasts, the collapse among the flames of races exhausted by the power of feeling, to the invading sound of enemy trumpets. The decadence is Sardanapalus lighting the fire in the midst of his women, it is Seneca declaiming poetry

[5]

as he opens his veins, it is Petronius masking his agony with flowers."

One can almost picture Verlaine speaking, or rather orating, about decadence, which in France at that time was very much a live word, though an exceedingly ambiguous one. One can see him reaching with trembling, nicotine-stained fingers for another absinthe (what drink better suggests our subject?), for which one of his adoring acolytes would have been delighted to pay, and then plunging off into another lurid literary travelogue. That hectic voluptuary, that impresario of evocation, was, as we shall see, partly responsible for the currency of "decadence" in the eighties in France.

Roman and Byzantine imagery had become attached to "decadence" only earlier in the century, but this penchant for the ancient world, in its more ferocious and flamboyant aspects, had been a French characteristic for a long time before that, and still is. The fascination of French writers and intellectuals for the colorful excesses of the classical past has had some unfortunate results. Flaubert's *Salammbô,* for instance, is one of the silliest, most indigestible novels by a writer of genius. But Flaubert's example has dissuaded no one in France. French authors go on rewriting the Greek plays and setting fictional parables in corrupt, sensual Alexandria or the Rome of the fires.

The word "decadence" has come down to us partly through writers such as Verlaine and Flaubert, who put their coloration on it, their stamp. Even today one cannot avoid seeing it at least in some manner through their eyes. But there is nevertheless a difference between their use of the word and ours. For all their hyperbole, they were serious about it, staking something on their interest. You would not have found them toying with "decadence" the way nearly all of us do these days, using it glibly, offhandedly, having encountered it in the *Zeitgeist*. If they could be said to have gone off the deep end sometimes, it was during a period when that was perhaps the only way to avoid running aground in the shallows.

"Decadence" was once a word that lived in the depths, under the pressure of extreme consciousness. Now it exists in the thin air of the pretense of extremity, a device for the imitation of spiritual or moral concern, or for mocking them. In a common formulation, *Variety* recently described an actor as "charming in a decadent sort of way," and Mick Jagger speaks of Paris as "conducive to having a good time. It's like Rome in that sense—decadent—which is nice, but . . ."

We nod; we know what is meant. But it's just there that the trouble begins. The ease with which the word comes to hand and tongue may conceal something important about language and life, and an exploration of its history, its biography, one might say, could be useful. How to go about it? How to deal with the pure unbounded abstractness of an entity that lacks a body, a soul, a specific place and time, except to pretend that it's a character in a story or a drama, or a mythological creature? The French are not at all bashful about practicing such anthropomorphism. Sartre, for instance, is always talking about poetry "reflecting on itself" or sensuality "undergoing a change of heart." Even in America, Lionel Trilling was able to make the careers of the words "Sincerity" and "Authenticity" seem like the life stories of a set of gifted, mistreated friends.

Actually, "hypostatization" or "reification" or, more familiarly, "personalization" are terms that are more to the point here than "anthropomorphism": to treat an abstraction such as a word or an idea as a thing, a living substance, a being. We do that with all our terminology of values: "the good," "happiness," "power," "perversion," and so on. Sometimes this process has rather droll consequences. Think of "smut," for example. One can see that reputed smudgy substance spreading over the land, staining our teen-agers a dirty brown, or else piling up in ramshackle warehouses, a species of tainted grain ready to infect the entire populace.

Like "sin" or "goodness," "decadence" has become a great temptation to the hypostatizer or reifier, particularly of the more vulgar, more impetuous sort. There is no question in such minds that decadence exists or at least has existed in specific places: ancient Rome, Alexandria, and Byzantium, of course, Paris of La Belle Époque, London of the Yellow Nineties, Istanbul, Berlin in the twenties, Hollywood, Fire Island. And it has clear lineaments: hooded eyelids and sardonic mouth, slender nervous fingers, and perhaps even a voice, one with a throaty, brandied sort of timbre. Is there any question about it? Is there any question about the existence of moral fiber? The world of clichés contains only answers.

A few years ago *The New York Times* offered the following item: "Senator Jacob Javits announced his candidacy for a fourth term yesterday, emphasizing his independence from President Nixon and castigating the 'moral and systemic decadence that has led us to the tragedy of Watergate.' "

The least significant thing about this quotation is that Watergate is being explained as the result of decadence instead of by the much simpler and more straightforward facts of evil and corruption. Much more disturbing, because it exhibits a blindness to the nature of language, a blindness we all share most of the time, is the notion of "castigating" decadence, shaking a stick at it as though it were a badly behaved dog, or a kind of Pied Piper tootling us to depravity.

Vulgar or not, personification appears to be unavoidable when one is trying to get at the life and potential death of a word, at its illnesses and recoveries, and especially at its insidious power, which all moral and spiritual terminology inevitably exerts over us. My own impulse, as I try to come to first grips with the subject of decadence—or rather, since nothing tangible has been discovered yet, the phenomenon of the word, the fact that it exists—is to describe it as a slippery customer, a chameleon changing color while you stare at it. In fact, that creature changes color *because* of your gaze.

This way of thinking about a word, which is something whose full implications the etymologist or linguistic scientist is likely to grasp (as the philosophers Nietzsche and Wittgenstein surely did), doubtless comes from an alarmed recognition of how hopeless it is to approach language as though it were settled, a matter of fixed dry equivalences, when it's really a matter, as we all secretly know, of flames, weathers, chemical actions, colors, and tides. If that seems excessive, too literary, then let us say that it's a matter of pressures, subtle quiddities, emanations. It may turn out to be impossible to *define* decadence, at least in any way satisfactory to people who believe in what William James derisively called the "calculable universe," those who trade in the nicest distinctions and live by separating one word or concept from another, sifters of the expressible or at any rate the thinkable.

Through a convention we all necessarily work by, the dictionary offers us and we accept "definitions" of so-called difficult or abstruse words, and it does this by referring us to the "meanings" of other words, simpler and more familiar ones, everything moving backward from the word in question to something more or less elemental. Right now, casting about for an example, I find the word "effulgent" coming to mind. The dictionary announces "radiant," which in turn yields "shining," "bright." There is no step back from that.

But "effulgent" remains idiosyncratic, inimitable, remote. It is not at all interchangeable with "bright," since what it has done is to have incorporated the latter word's thinner substance while revealing only its own origin in Latin, that is to say its historical background but not its present life. The only way we can discover the actuality of a word defined by reference to a simpler one is through poetry, or some other kind of imaginative literary action.

And so one has to use the dictionary in the quest for "decadence" but the best that can be hoped for is to be told what words this one is related to, what verbal neighborhoods the fugitive has been known to frequent, who its cronies and accomplices are. I think it better, though, to start somewhere nearer to hand. It might be useful to bring "decadence" up to the eye, imagining it as three-dimensional, a palpability concerned to be known, or at any rate not ill disposed to being seen.

> Life is an old casino in a park.
> The bills of the swans are flat upon the ground.
> A most desolate wind has chilled Rouge-Fatima.
> And a grand decadence settles down like cold.
> —Wallace Stevens, "Academic Discourse at Havana"

These are mysterious lines. One can sense the *effect* of the word "decadence" among the physical images, but can't really know its meaning. This situation repeats itself whenever the word is used outside formal cultural discussion, a matter we shall come to later. But to open oneself to the word's emanations is a start.

There is a sense of it as preserved in archaic distance, one of those words like "courtesan" or "bacchanalia" that we keep around as verbal relics of an erstwhile sinfulness this side of full, serious evil. Before any specific associations arise "decadence" gives off a feeling of age, of superseded behavior, something almost quaint and even faintly comical. Going further, allowing this strange and marginal word to declare itself more fully, one can detect in it a quality of languor, of debility, a suggestion of repletion but also of continual striving toward pleasure of a bizarre, peripheral kind. There is a sense about it of intent, if constricted, consciousness and extreme refinement: narrowed eyes, tapping fingers, sensual choices made exactingly among uncommon fragrances and rare colors, in half-light. There is nothing violent or barbaric about it, nothing so extreme. Genghis Khan, as one historian has written, was not a decadent.

Another and related sense of transgression clings to the word. But it has to do with taboos violated not out of surging passion or grim philosophy but out of cynicism or what one might call a surfeit of the licit. One thinks of an irritated ennui stealing over those of the rich or powerful who don't feel themselves bound by prevailing tastes or standards, or even regard it as an obligation to break with them. And finally there is a nuance of distemper, of being out of sorts, neurasthenia producing an exquisite itch for whose relief no habitual or straightforward remedy will do.

This is a useful summary, an educated approach, as far as

it goes. But it is all too vague and abstract, too conscious and reasonable. I would like to try an experiment in free association, springing the word "decadence" on myself as though for therapeutic purposes.

I lie down. Words come: "honor," "family," "survival," "decadence" . . . elegant opium dens with suave, slinky hostesses; bedrooms with mirrored ceilings and black satin sheets on the emperor-sized beds; women in high heels, black stockings, and garter belts; Marlene Dietrich in *The Blue Angel* with Emil Jannings crowing like a rooster; bathrooms with purple or zebra-striped tiling; Tangiers; Pompeii; a Black Mass; Turkish pashas in their playrooms; *Les Fleurs du mal;* a drag-queen costume ball; a voyeur with expensive binoculars trained on the windows of a girls' boarding-school dormitory; Oscar Wilde and the green carnation; Onassis' yacht with paparazzi snapping pictures from the shore; a Roman orgy with fan-waving Nubian slaves and crimson wine trickling out of the corners of heavy sensual mouths; Regine's; jeweled money belts; fruit-flavored douches and edible panties.

One finds it difficult to believe that such a cluster of images and associations differs too widely in its general import from what would be arrived at by anyone familiar with the history of the word or at least with its current usage. The litany is mostly sexual—or at least open to erotic interpretation—and heavily literary. That is to say, almost none of the images and scenes derive from direct experience of my own, but rather from creations in the realm of culture, that dimension of invented or dramatized existence.

Even such "facts" as opium dens or Tangiers are not truly available to me except through a screen of fiction, of imaginary action, and this would be true even if I were to prowl the streets of that North African city and stumble into a scene of astonishing depravity, or if I were to settle down with a pipeful of hashish on a luxurious sofa in a magenta-colored flock-walled room in Hongkong or Macao. I would respond to or continue to seek for qualities of sensual excitation or fulfillment of which I had first become aware through one or another kind of "tale." This is an important clue, I think. Like so many other categories of the "abnormal," decadence makes itself known to us, at least in the beginning, in the form of a legend.

In *L'Ève Future*, Villiers de l'Isle-Adam, whose career was at its height during the so-called Decadent Period in France at the end of the last century, wrote the following characteristic description of a femme fatale:

Beneath the horizontal immobility of the long eyebrows, two dark blue eyes under languid Hindu lids, two magnificent eyes laden with dreams, spread about her a transforming magic over all things in heaven and on earth. He saturated with unknown charms the fateful features of that face whose beauty was unforgettable . . . the cruel flared nostrils which quivered at the scent of danger, the mouth tinged with a gleam of blood, the chin of a silent despoiler.

This is a "decadent" portrait, but does the quality, like beauty, lie in the subject or in the creator? The problem will continue to be present, complicating the pursuit of meaning in regard to "decadence." To describe is often to attribute, to confer what is not physically there. But in any case Villiers' woman is a creature entirely of imagination, a literary being, and comes to us exhibiting decadence in one of its reputed forms. Later we shall perhaps see how *all* the forms in which we think we detect the phenomenon of decadence are products of the word's prior uses and not stable realities of the objective world.

There is something else to be noticed about the list of associations we have been accumulating—the behavior, taste, and imaginative disposition it reveals may be beyond the normal or conventional, but not shockingly so; there is nothing really vile or unimaginable here. The murderer, the torturer of children, or the great betrayer like Judas is in a moral condition distinguished from that of decadence (if indeed decadence has anything to do with morality) by his absolute break with the acceptable. Dostoevsky understood as much as anybody ever has about distinctions of this kind. For example, Raskolnikov, in his hermetic criminality (think of how a moment after the murder of the old woman he feels himself to be in a silent, glacial world) is an entirely different species of moral being from, say, Nastasya Filippovna, whose testing of her suitors by flinging the packet of rubles on the fire, in *The Idiot,* would seem to be a superb example of what we like to think of as a decadent act.

The formulation might then be made: however extreme so-called decadent behavior might be, it retains its connections to the unproscribed. One can think of it as a more or less distant segment of an arc whose beginning is fully within our ordinary sphere of appetite and action. The Russian theologian-critic Vyacheslav Ivanov described decadence as the "feeling, at once oppressive and exalting, of being the last of a series." Whatever the hyperbole here, the point is that if decadence exists at all, it isn't self-contained or an abrupt departure from standards. It is not a break but some sort of extension. One might offer a tentative definition (keeping in mind that the description is of an idea, not a proven reality): decadence is a moribund or late—not necessarily "last"—corrupted stage of one or another aspect of civilized existence, a stage, also, in its widest application, of a civilization itself.

This is the meaning obscured behind all those aphrodisiac images of studied sensuality and refined vice that the word first presents to us; and it is also the meaning most familiar to us in formal cultural history. There it refers to specific periods and styles in art and literature that are supposed to have been marked by debility and lack of original force in comparison to the "health" of immediately preceding epochs: Mannerist painting; various types of Rococo; the writing and art of the late Roman Empire; certain fiction, poetry, and painting of the late nineteenth century in Europe. Applied this way, the designation releases ideas of excess, loss of vigor, tyranny at the hands of the past (a despotism acquiesced in, however), a concern with manner at the expense of substance, a hunger for the deviant as a positive principle. It is not, after all, such a great theoretical distance from these notions to the life of the word in popular idiom now.

"What decadence in literature really means," Arthur Symons wrote in 1887 in his *Essay on Meredith,* "is that learned corruption of language by which style ceases to be organic and becomes, in the pursuit of some new expressiveness or beauty, deliberately abnormal." This is no doubt accurate, by which I mean it is true to what was thought about decadence in scholarly circles at the time and for the most part still is. But in the face of the naked word such studiousness and sobriety are difficult to maintain against the gravitational pull of the word away from the conceptual or evaluative and toward the fleshly, the flagrantly pictorial. One result of this tropism of "decadence" toward the sensual is that the word loses any status it might have had as a moral, spiritual, or cultural term and takes on the bristling physiognomy of an expletive. This is an outcome we are familiar with in verbal matters. We need to give life to our abstractions; we can't go around with such gases in our heads. Abstractions make science possible, it's true, but they tend to bully affective life into confusion and incoherence.

This means that there is a price to pay whenever we try to locate abstractions in energetic, specific reality. Like so many words that originate in grand categories of the mind or imagination, "decadence" has been debased into a label, a wholly imprecise means of evocation or identification. More than that, one can see in the process a certain borrowing of prestige or size, something that happens when we call a man a "prince" or speak of a physical action as "sheer poetry" or remark that there's "the devil to pay." "Philosophy" is an obvious word of this kind: the downward path is from the "rational investigation of the truths of knowledge, being, or conduct" to a car dealer's principles of salesmanship. "Tragedy" is another: from the plays of Aeschylus and Sophocles to a fallen soufflé, a lost dog, or Watergate.

We indulge in such random and inappropriate usages with "decadence" these days, applying it with waning disapprobation and a more or less furtive fascination to eating habits, interior decoration, styles of dress, and of course many crepuscular sexual practices and tastes. Or else, less stylishly, we wield it moralistically, brandishing it at the most dissimilar phenomena: corrupt politics, the mores of the jet set and hard-core skin flicks, topless waitresses and gold toothpicks. What "decadence" is almost never any longer used to describe—as a little research will indicate it once so soberly and almost exclusively was—are broad cultural movements or the conditions of life of entire societies; except, that is to say, in the case of Chinese or *soi-disant* Maoists' characterizations of bourgeois or capitalist societies and even of the Soviet Union.

The New Decadence has been the subject of dozens of admiring—or at least far from disapproving—magazine articles, the kind by which editors fulfill their desperate obligation to be "with it." A writer on food resists the temptation, she tells us, to indulge in a restaurant's "gorgeously decadent" desserts. *Playboy* runs a report on the opulent world cruise of the liner *France* under the title "One More Crack at Glorious Decadence." A far-out rock-theatrical group calls itself, with oxymoronic flair, the Decadent Poor. Sally Bowles' encomium, "divine decadence, darling," passes into the chitchat at Maxwell's Plum. It is all something of a joke, a cuteness about moral being and behavioral risks; it's a bit of camp about what was surely a troubled spiritual condition that some of our predecessors took pains to try to identify.

"I enjoy decadence and I also enjoy democracy," Kenneth Tynan says in regard to life in Germany under the Weimar Republic. "Germany then," he goes on, "was about as decadent as it's humanly possible to be, but it was also fairly democratic. It even seemed to be moving toward socialism, and that would have been ideal—socialism and self-gratification at the same time."

Chic and obtuse at the same time, ignorant of history (we will return to Germany in the twenties as a purported hotbed of decadence) as well as of language, remarks like this perpetuate and deepen many of our confusions. And it is just such popularizing, slumming commentators who use "decadence" as though it were beyond question, a settled matter. When Pauline Kael continually links "decadence" with fascism, as though they were somehow nearly synonymous, she does so on the basis of no historical understanding or even acquaintance but simply because moviemakers, in their own ignorance, have made the silly connection, its grounds presumably being flamboyant uniforms and stiff, monumental architecture.

The surprising revival of "decadence" is a matter, it would seem, of undiscriminating fashion and odd, exceedingly odd, nostalgia. For the tight-lipped, who reflexively continue to employ it as a pejorative, the word has very little to recommend it these days. You can feel the condemnatory power steadily draining out of it—except in academic circles, lagging as usual. Even Kael's vision of it is as something rather enjoyable, something with flair. More and more it is merely one of the flashy new indices to taste and behavior which ostensibly relieve boredom and provide a route into new "experience" by trafficking (not at all grimly) in various taboos. That these latter are in most cases in the process of disappearing is of course to the point; active taboos tend to cow journalists and people who think like journalists.

One must add to this that if there are any true decadents

among us, whatever their condition might mean, they don't use the word about themselves. At the moment it's an onlooker's term, as were in their various ways and times words like "madcap" or "philanderer" or "hippie."

Thus far, in examining usages and associations, we have come scarcely any distance toward a meaning for the word. And although the matter of usage is at the center of the cultural mission of this inquiry—to track down, confront, cut off all escape routes from, and finally badger "decadence" into revealing as exhaustively as possible what it is and has been and may become as a verbal force—the operation requires that formal meanings be considered, and all the more in a case where so rakish, protean, and mystifying a word has had its meanings so widely undermined or successively abandoned.

To begin with, we can say (and it will be the burden of this book to establish) that "decadence" is an unstable word and concept whose significations and weights continually change in response to shifts in morals, social and cultural attitudes, and even technology. In this regard it resembles "progress," one of its rough antonyms. There is nothing surprising in such a fate, one shared with all our terminology of value and behavior. One has only to think of "the good," "the beautiful," "obscenity," "respectability," or, most central of all, "morality" itself. Historically, all have veered away from any fixed condition capturable by the dictionary, and they continue to do so, moving to what is wanted of them by particular minds and at particular moments. These words are the victims of, yet also the conspirators in, our treacherous subjectivity. For as they move to establish our immediate intentions they exert a counterpull in the direction of a reality they had previously indicated, they revive something once achieved in the description of the moral or spiritual life, which has been institutionalized, so to speak, in our processes of thought.

To investigate the historical career of the word and concept "decadence" (a rather different thing from looking into so-called historical decadences themselves, where the assumption is of something known, demonstrable) is to bring to light an especially dramatic instance of what we already know or have suspected about language, but which we habitually suppress: that it is as much our master as our tool. For words, nearly all of which exist before we do (new words in most fully developed languages are almost always of a technical kind or are appropriated from other languages, like "weekend" being taken into French or "détente" into English), compel us toward that prior life. What is "decadent" now is at least in part what has been thought of as decadent at some earlier time, just as the "good" and the "sinful" make themselves known to us trailing those Greek or Judeo-Christian accouterments which go to fill out the forms of our moral and spiritual education, however informal or even accidental that might be.

That moral and spiritual ideas exhibit both change and stability—good and evil, for example, perpetually shifting their ground while retaining some intellectual or ideological core—is a commonplace. But something else is at stake in the area of verbal reality. A word, after all, is a sign for a thing, an action, a quality, or a condition, and signs have a way of breaking loose from their fixed positions or of being uprooted from them. When time, duration, enters in as a protracted influence the word as sign may come to find itself at a great remove from the actuality it was once employed to indicate. It would be like a piece of wreckage with a ship's name on it floating away from a sunken hulk, or a marker in the desert pointing to a vanished city. The word retains a reality, a fragment of consciousness clings to it, but there is nothing "real" to which it now corresponds. Between these two conditions—of relic and drifting sign—it may be possible to see "decadence" pursuing its strange career.

The catalogues of most of the great libraries in America will direct you from "decadence" to "degeneration" (where the most prominent listing is of a shabby, disreputable, but well-known 1898 tome with that title by Max Nordau) or on occasion to "debasement," "corruption," or "degradation"— i.e., *The Degradation of the Democratic Dogma* by Brooks Adams. But the only book entitled *Decadence* in the three or four large libraries I visited is by the British philosopher C. E. M. Joad, to whom we will return later.

In the same irritating way, Webster's New Dictionary of Synonyms refers one from "decadence" to "backwards," under which heading the words "retrograde," "regressive," and "retrogressive" are thoughtfully distinguished from one another while "decadence" keeps its counsel somewhere in the background.

Except in the area of etymology, regular dictionaries are not much help either, as they aren't for most words of subtle spiritual or moral import. They will tell you that the word does not derive from "decade," as one might have vaguely thought it did (the plausibility here being some sort of affliction setting in every ten years or so, a midgenerational fever), but from *decadere,* Latin for "to fall down or away." The word seems to have come into English, as have so many terms for delicately discriminated states of civilized awareness and behavior, through French (*décadence*) via Medieval Latin (*decadentia*), the roughly coeval Spanish and Italian equivalents being *decadencia* and *decadenza* respectively.

Depending on which authority one consults, the word's first recorded uses in these European languages are in the early thirteenth, fourteenth, or fifteenth centuries, the dispute centering on when the word was first employed in any sense recognizable to us. The first use in English I have been able to find is in a work of 1549 called, in the Oxford English Dictionary, the *Complete* (or *Compleat*) *Scotsman,* from which the following sentence is quoted: "My triumphant stait is succumbit in decadens." As late as 1782 William Bailey's Etymological English Dictionary gave the word as "decadency," a variant that persisted informally for many years after that and may still be employed in odd pedantic quarters. ("Decadentism" is another variant that has been in use at times.)

Definitions have remained extraordinarily constant since Bailey gave his readers "a falling down, decay, declension," and Samuel Johnson's Dictionary some twenty-five years before had laconically offered "decay," "fall." The current Random House Dictionary of the English Language is a bit more expansive: "The act of falling into an inferior condition or state; decay; deterioration." The modern French, Spanish, Italian, German, and several other European dictionaries I have consulted are all in agreement with the English ones in presenting "decay" as the primary meaning, with "deterioration" as the secondary one.

Not until the later part of the nineteenth century did the dictionary examples of the word's use begin to take on the rather narrowly moral and specifically behavioral connotations to which we have become accustomed. But even during this period it is possible to come upon some surprising reversals or misapplications of what had been the generally accepted sense of the term. "This process is said to prevent the decadence of the hair," declares a health columnist in the *Birmingham Weekly Post* for November 15, 1884. And in a literary essay in the *Saturday Review* for April 23, 1892, one is startled to see the following bit of praise: "It is very prettily and decadently written."

The late 1880s and '90s also find both the noun and the adjective coming to have reference for the first time to something objective and more or less precisely delimited. One strand of formal culture in France and England at the time, along with modes of activity not necessarily artistic but wishing to appear so, conferred upon the words their occasional upper-case *D*. "Decadent: One of a group of French and English writers of the latter part of the nineteenth century whose works were characterized by great refinement or subtlety of style and by a marked tendency toward the artificial or abnormal in content."—The Random House Dictionary of the English Language.

This dictionary is not quite factually accurate (to say nothing of its schoolmarmish and philistine aesthetics) in that it confines its definition of decadence to writers, when the truth, of course, is that painters, sculptors, and other artists, as well as a great many artist types and artists *manqués,* were accorded the designation or appropriated it to themselves. In any case, the eighties and nineties of the last

century were the first period in which "decadence" and "decadents" were used as proper nouns and remain the only one
in which such usage was widespread.

"We're very decadent, you know," a bored-looking young
man tells a reporter at a discotheque. "But if we weren't
decadent, we'd be something else." "Decadence rules!" a
rock singer announces. "It's so lovely, so unlimited, so
natural." A review of a book on the Rolling Stones speaks
of the "lyrical decadence" of one of their tours. A talk-show
host thinks *Playboy* and Hugh Hefner decadent but adds
that theirs is a "benevolent" kind. On a more complex level a
critic says of a novelist that his "use of decadence" is skillful
and absorbing.

The strange, illiterate, and hyperbolic uses proliferate and
are not confined to the professionally or temperamentally
au courant. We are all in the same situation of ignorance and
gullibility in regard to this peculiar word. Not exactly
"world-weary" or "self-indulgent" or "ultrarefined" or
"overcivilized"; not "debauchery," "effeteness," "depravity,"
"hedonism," or "luxuriousness"; certainly not simply "decay"
or "degeneration" or "retrogression," "decadence" seems to
gather in all these meanings and implications and to exist
precariously and almost cabalistically beyond them. Its origins
buried under successive drifts of culture, its resonances somehow greatly out of keeping with its putative formal tasks, it
recommends itself to us now, or forces itself upon our attention, like some old and intricately specialized object of
vaguely exotic use. Part of the language and even increasing
its narrow sway, it could, if it would, perhaps teach us some-

thing about language by its strange survival and resistance to clear meaning.

But a word doesn't exist within language alone and so cannot be sought simply within that realm, the way an animal, or a flower, can in its kingdom. Words exist in consciousness, the dominion of mind, which is made up partly of language and partly of that zone of the unexpressed, or not yet expressed, compounded of nonverbal memory, perceptions, intuitions, and sheer sensory experiences, all of which is continually thrusting toward utterance or dropping back into the forgotten or suppressed.

Language is of course in a sense a game, as Wittgenstein described it, a game in which words are counters; the rules are forever changing but the intent remains constant. And that is to try to control experience artificially, in an action that in drawing upon the magical power of naming gains provisional control over the world.

The key word here is "provisional," a condition of the temporary satisfaction of a need or desire. We live in a succession of such temporary fulfillments, such temporariness in general, but language is one force that works to obscure this. Its own continuity seems absolute, and we borrow this seeming permanence in order to escape the anguish that a full recognition of the provisional nature of existence would induce in us.

But words live, as we do, in time, and can escape neither its ravages nor its deceptions. Words in time, words with histories: one intellectual problem is that of bringing such verbal presences and histories into coherence with our own. That is what I want to try to do with "decadence," a word, like certain others, the implications of whose fate seem to me greatly significant of wider, deeper matters than can ever be seen from inside language itself. In that place the temptation is to take what's at hand; and intellectual degradation is at least as near to us as wisdom.

2

Friedrich Nietzsche ONCE WROTE IN REGARD to decadence that it was a "problem" that "has preoccupied me more" than any other; indeed he devoted great portions of *The Will to Power* and *The Case of Wagner* to the question, as well as touching on it on hundreds of occasions in other books and essays. William Butler Yeats once lyrically described the so-called Decadent Movement of the 1890's as a reflection of "the autumns of the body." In his long treatise on the subject, C. E. M. Joad interpreted decadence in a peculiarly abstract and passionless way, writing that it "is a sign of man's tendency to misread his position in the universe, to take a view of his status and prospects more exalted than the facts warrant and to conduct his societies and to plan his future on the basis of this misunderstanding." On a less lofty plane, although mysteriously enough, we are told that Colette, in an aphoristic mood, once commented to her husband Maurice Goudeket that "suffering is the great decadence."

All this is imposing testimony to the long life and seeming vigor of the word, if also to the puzzling diversity of its uses. Yet Baudelaire, who, rightly or not, seems to incarnate the most profound aspects of what we think of as decadence, the way Oscar Wilde does the more frivolous ones, gave as his opinion that "decadence" was "a very convenient word for ignorant pedagogues; a vague word behind which we shelter our laziness and lack of curiosity regarding the law." In *The Idea of History*, R. G. Collingwood wrote that "this distinction between ideas of primitiveness, periods of greatness, and periods of decadence is not and never can be historically true." Anatole France said once that "I have heard about this 'decadence'; I don't believe in it." And Ernest Renan, a younger contemporary of Baudelaire, asserted that "there is no decadence from the point of view of humanity. Decadence is a word that ought to be definitively banished from history."

No decadence? Does this mean that there is no objective reality to which this noun points, or is it that there is no justification for using it to indicate something that indeed exists? Whichever it is, if we want to "banish" the word, as Renan proposed, how do we go about it? Do we hold a trial, hear evidence and character witnesses, retire to the jury room, pronounce a verdict, and then watch the guilty one, its poor tattered vague possessions wrapped up in an Art Nouveau bundle on a stick, or thrown into a suitcase held together with cord and bearing stickers from Monte Carlo, Marrakesh, and the liner *Ile de France,* trudge toward the designated border station with an occasional melancholy backward glance? And what land will accept this exile?

Renan knew as well as anyone that words cannot be banished from language, forcibly ejected; the experience of bodies such as the French Academy, in their attempts to protect languages from incursions and root out unwanted presences, is all the proof that's needed. Words may die, of course, pass out of usage and turn into relics—"courtesan," "airship"—but this is never the result of anyone's decision. In almost all cases such linguistic events are the consequence of a change in actuality, the result being that words become emptied of significance, which is to say they are no longer *signs* of anything still thought to be actual. But this is exactly what brings about the problem of "decadence" as a word. Since it has remained in the language, indeed is experiencing a vigorous new life, it must, we have to assume, refer to something real.

This is a trap. "Decadence" is a *name,* and in regard to the relations between names and things we are still in a realm of pre-science. In *The Act of Creation,* Arthur Koestler writes:

In the mentality of primitives, the person and his name are magically related. In Eastern religions, evocations of the names of Deities—the recital of mantras—fulfill a magic function . . . This attitude lingers on in medieval philosophy (Realists vs. Nominalists); in all forms of magic, and, more covertly, in modern science—in the unconscious belief that words like gravity, entelechy or electro-magnetic "field," etc. somehow have an explanatory value *an sich.* Such is the power of verbal symbols to focus attention that it confers on hazy concepts *in statu nascendi* the appearance of hard, tangible concreteness and "gives to airy nothingness a local habitation and a name." The name is then experienced as a self-evident explanation.

The malady is even more widespread than Koestler thinks. It is very difficult for us to accept the idea that the existence of a word does not guarantee a reality, palpable or abstract, to which it refers. The exceptions, of course, are archaisms, words that we recognize as "dead" and therefore inoperative in the real world, and nonsense words, ones that are made up from the elements of ordinary "useful" language and that testify only to the existence of nonsense (and so, it would seem, to a reality after all). The only time we have substantial difficulty with the inherent identity of words and what they exist to designate is in the presence of a foreign language of which we are ignorant. Think of the odd sensation you would have if, not knowing French, you heard a French person utter the word *tasse,* say, and then learned through an interpreter or a dictionary that it means cup. It may *mean* cup but it isn't cup; "cup" is cup.

Eugene Ionesco made a great deal of comic capital out of this and other truths about our shackled relation to language in early plays like *The Bald Soprano,* where all the members of a large family are named Bobby Watson, and *The Lesson,* in which the same word has a different meaning depending on whether it's spoken in Madrid or Paris and where a professor of language stabs a girl to death with the *word* "knife," the French word for it.

But ordinarily, safe within our own habitual language, the one we are implicitly and otherwise led to believe from the beginning is the only *real* tongue, we have no problems. The French, as we know, are especially given to linguistic jingoism. Once in the caves of Altamira I heard a Frenchman, the only one in the group of tourists, repeat loudly to himself in his own language the Spanish guide's Spanish patter, as though the information couldn't be real until it had been translated. Ordinarily, I say, we accept without question the indivisible relation of words to things, proceeding comfortably enough in our daily affairs (although frequently lapsing into hypostatization or reification in our political, philosophical, and spiritual exercises) to use words for indicating aspects of reality, for naming what lies before us, for making distant things present, restoring dead things to provisional life, and bringing invisible things into view in the mind's so-called eye.

Now, decadence is an invisible thing or entity (although

Renan's and Anatole France's disbelief in its existence could scarcely be due to that). This is not to say it doesn't have manifestations—if it refers to anything real, that is—but only that it's a noun of condition, not corporeality; it denotes a category in the dimension of activity or behavior, not an object. If it were an object, however exotic, like a vademecum or a stomacher, let's say, or a creature such as a marabou or manatee, all we would have to do, *theoretically,* is to search for it throughout the world, and while if we didn't find it we wouldn't be absolutely certain of its nonexistence, we would be sure enough for all practical purposes. In that case it would be a rumor.

The deep problem about words of evaluation, judgmental words, is that they impose themselves on objects and phenomena that already have other names and thus other identities. All adjectives and adverbs function this way, to be sure, but we don't have much trouble with them except in the sphere of values. There is nothing problematic about a blue house (except of course as a matter of taste), but a *bawdy* house? As for nouns, those primary materials of our verbal world, they become dangerous precisely when they are abstract and doubly so when they pronounce judgment. "Steamship," for example, is what it is, a vessel that moves through the sea by means of energy generated by heated water; "food" is what is ingested by an organism and nourishes it.

But "sin," "happiness," "obscenity," "honor," and so on? These words can't exist by themselves (except in Plato's ideal realm, the first formal structure of reification that we have record of in human thinking) but are forever straining to attach themselves, as adjectives for the most part, to palpable objects and activities, imitating the way paint strains toward a surface or a button toward a buttonhole.

A result of this is that many words of this kind spread their warping, distorting or, at the least, confusing presence all over the palpable. "Sex," for instance, is what it is (whatever it may be), but when "sin" takes it into its embrace, as has happened so often in the past and still does, a strange darkening of the word occurs. (The same thing happens if you conjoin "promiscuous" to "sex" or, it's almost too obvious to note, "sex" to "fiend.") "Money" is clear enough, but when "success" surrounds it and absorbs it the moral universe, as well as the universe of meanings, is shaken and confused. "Sin," "success," "dignity," "degradation," "health," "superiority," "guilt," and so on: this is a language of wish, fear, hope, arbitrary decisions, a lexicon of the doubtful, perhaps even the unreal.

Is "decadence" a word of the same order, even though it appears to be so much more specific, to have bones and surfaces about it? I suspect it is, but the job of justifying this suspicion lies ahead of us. After all, the word exists, and its myriad associations in the outer as well as the psychic world are far from easy to dislodge. If, like Renan, you try to wish the word out of existence, those black satin sheets, those women in garter belts, and that decor of Berlin in the twenties press you to account for them; ancient Rome clears its hoarse throat. A word for lazy, incurious persons, Baudelaire said of it, a word for pedagogues, and, one might add, perhaps also for the pretentious, the undiscriminating, the tactless and shallow. But this is getting ahead of our argument, as well as of "decadence," which at the moment calmly awaits the effort to prove that it is not the oblique, mauve- and tangerine-colored, fine-boned, weary, subtly menacing, insidiously destructive, and enervating creature or organism to which so much recognition has been granted—that in fact it is not anything at all.

A note: There is a sense in which abstract, judgmental words of the kind I have been talking about become more or less neutralized in a usage that is narrowly denotative: for example, "sin" when it refers to what Catholic or other religious doctrine holds to be evil, or "success" when it simply describes the desired outcome of some specific task or challenge. I shall be using "decadence" occasionally in these ways, to refer to the word's existence in other minds or mouths, or in its narrow technical meaning as a "falling down" or "away."

Moreover, the word has had a life in at least three different realms, the political, the cultural, and the moral, with an ascending degree of murk and inappropriateness, which reflects the progressively more problematic natures of the orders of reality in the series. I shall try to keep clearly before us what order I am investigating or discussing at any moment.

This won't be easy. The fact is that "decadence" is embedded in the thickest, most tangled linguistic and historical contexts, and so there is nothing to do but plunge into those jungles on its trail. And yet there is really only one jungle, I suspect; history is as much the record of language as of anything else. It may even be, in some terrifying but also perhaps liberating sense, *only* the record of language. In his play *Kaspar,* Peter Handke has gone so far as to call history "a story of sentences." What if it is really something even more elemental: a story, a tale with an ending, of words?

Although "decadence" is a word of Latin origin, there is no record of its having been in use in Roman times. It first appears in medieval Latin early in the second millennium of the Christian era. Yet we closely associate it with the Romans, taking from their ostensible political and social histories, as Rémy de Gourmont has observed, our conception of historical decadence itself, and from the vicissitudes of their art and literature our primary idea of aesthetic decadence as well. More immediately and more vulgarly we ground many of our notions of what we might call "behavioral" decadence on what we have been taught of Roman practices, on the indulgences and excesses of its upper classes and the flamboyant, despairing immorality of rulers like Nero and Caligula.

But though the word itself was not used by the Romans, so strongly has modern consciousness been impressed by its evocative and categorical power that it has been widely and anachronistically employed in regard to Rome, being most often used to translate what the Roman historians and chroniclers, in so far as they were referring to the same things, expressed in other terms. Chief among these were *vacillatio* and *inclinatio,* both of which words were generally descriptive nouns without specific moral references and certainly without the sexual connotations so much in vogue today. Both dealt with what was thought to be evidence of public or national "decline," what was taken to be regression, a backward movement of morals (in the largest public sense), of manners, and, most important, of social and political reality. The loss of various kinds of power or control, and above all of continuity, was what was central to their usage. In the second century A.D. *inclinatio* took on an additional reference to aesthetic matters, in an attempt to explain an apparent loss of skill by painters and sculptors.

Despite their easily apprehended literal meanings, these words are as mysterious in their own right as is "decadence" itself. A leaning, a wavering; the images are those of something being undermined or subverted: a tower with a crack at its base, a rudderless ship, a tremor in the earth. Both words emerge from a world of consciousness that we can sense as having been peculiarly vulnerable to the unknown, metaphysically tremulous, full of intimations of large inexorable powers inimical to human life and institutions. Especially to institutions: to a very much greater degree than is true of us the Greeks and Romans saw the self as having been shaped by and held in being by traditional means, public in origin.

Before going further into what the ancient world may have thought about itself, however, it might be useful to consider for a moment what we think of it, for it's our habit to impose on the past what the past itself might never have thought or experienced. In his study of the nature of history as an intellectual discipline, a science, R. G. Collingwood has argued that the only real subject for the historian is previous *thought,* and that history is precisely the rethinking of what was once thought. The inability of a historian to enter the mind of the past results in his preoccupation with its remains and hence in interpretations based on external "facts." And facts by themselves can tell us only what we now think of them, very little of what they once meant.

The conventional way to think of Roman history, for example, is to arrange it along a progression of large facts, to assume that Rome was "founded," that it "developed," that it grew powerful, reached a condition of repletion and marvelous self-assurance, entered into an irresistible (or at any rate unresisted) state of decline, and finally "fell." If we owe this language chiefly to Gibbon, he can only be held partly responsible for our tendency to imagine the fall as having happened all at once (in the year 410, for those of us who lack the wiser historian's sense of loose ends) and with graphic particularity: a gigantic statue with a weakened base is toppled by a barbarian mob.

The image is immensely revealing of our way of looking at the past. In our minds ancient societies and civilizations (quite recent ones for that matter; the Victorian era is a case in point) are always monoliths composed of tight sets of a few frozen characteristics. Egypt is slow, hooded, hieratic; Greece is open, wise, sunlit; Rome is harshly splendid, cold, finally rotten at the core. There is a reduction at work in this to something narrow and thus graspable, as though we feel the need to turn civilizations into a typology resembling that of the characters of melodrama.

There is a melodramatic quality, too, in our thinking of historical epochs (though not our own; who can recognize an epoch from the middle of it?) as being analogous to the course of a human life: birth, youth, maturity, old age, and death. Among the intellectual distortions this anthropomorphism produces is that of endowing history with a sense of fatality for which, as any clear-headed investigation will reveal, there is no real justification except a literary one. And in fact it was Gibbon, that novelist struggling with the more sober demands of the historian's profession, who gave in regard to Rome the most sonorous expression of that idea of inevitability, of events having to have been the way they were, which so strangely and beautifully consoles us in fiction but for which history provides no proof. "The story of its ruin," Gibbon wrote, "is simple and obvious; and instead of enquiring why the Roman Empire was destroyed we should rather be surprised that it had subsisted for so long . . . The whole stupendous fabric yielded to the pressure of its own weight."

As a shrewd recent writer on the last centuries of imperial Rome, F. W. Wallbank, has noted, this explanation is no explanation at all; the fabric yielding to itself is a metaphor, a literary conceit. But at least, Wallbank goes on to observe, Gibbon's "formulation . . . broke with all cyclical, mystical-biological and metaphysical theories of decline, and stated clearly the 'naturalistic' view." Among the Romans themselves such theories were what the words *vacillatio* and *inclinatio* participated in with all their opaque mysterious presence. If we can really call them "theories"; they are closer to intuitions, hunches after looking up at the sky.

But the really strange thing, the mystery behind the mysteriousness, was why such notions or intuitions should have existed at all, or at least why decline should have been felt with all the forcefulness and specificity of an observable phenomenon, a fateful, inexorable one to boot, and why it should have been felt so extraordinarily early in Roman civilization, as well as in so many others. Did ancient civilizations really "decline," go from ruddy health to states of senescence, of "decadence"? And, if such were the case, of what did that decadence consist?

That civilization was moving in reverse, human institutions exhibiting signs of slippage and erosion while the world itself grew less and less amenable to mankind, less of a "home," was actually experienced long before Roman society had any identity. At the dawn of formal Greek consciousness and expression, for example, we find Hesiod unable to bear the spectacle of what he saw as contemporary decline, and though neither he nor later Greek writers had any evocative terms for it, decline or regression was perpetually before their "eyes" and on their minds.

Such a pessimistic reading of the present is of course what lies behind all myths of golden ages. In every early civilization of which we have knowledge—Indian, Chinese, Egyptian, Mesopotamian, as well as Greek—such legends of an earlier "better" time are to be found in abundance, and are always accompanied by laments over the reduced or maimed quality of life in the present. But it would be hard to find a true, solid, inspiriting myth of a golden future. This would come into being only with the advent of Christianity, for which the future, however, was not to be of this world.

The complaints of classical writers about the inferiority of the present to the past reveal a continually widening range of reference. Plato wrote in *The Republic,* as though it were a matter of common knowledge, that the men who came before us were happier than we are and closer to the gods. Centuries later, in imperial Roman times, Horace complained: "What does not ruinous time degrade? The age of our parents, inferior to that of our grandparents, brought forth ourselves, who are more worthless still and destined to have children still more corrupt." In the same era Lucretius indulged himself in a long, detailed jeremiad:

And now already our age is decayed. The earth grows weary and can scarce create small animals—earth that once created all the generations of men and gave birth to the gigantic bodies of beasts—the same earth once created spontaneously for mortal men the golden corn and the joyful vines . . . and now . . . they will scarcely grow with all our labor . . . the old plowman sighs often, bewails his fruitless labor and compares the present time with times past, praising often the good fortune of his father . . . everything slowly decays, marching toward the tomb, exhausted by the ancient lapse of time.

Several centuries after this, in the year A.D. 250, at a time when the classical world was well on the way toward what we think of as its "end," St. Cyprian, who was to become a martyr for Christianity eight years later, renewed Lucretius' dirge and extended its scope:

The world has now grown old and does not abide in that strength in which it formerly stood . . . In winter there is no longer enough rain to feed the crops; in summer the sun is no longer hot enough to ripen the fruit . . . the land remains without farmers; the sea without sailors; the armies without soldiers. There is no more innocence in politics, and justice in the courts, and mastership in the arts; and discipline in moral behavior.

Cyprian's lament, although the product of an especially apocalyptic mind for which the imminent end of the world was an article of religious faith, is nevertheless representative, a compendium of the judgments any sensitive person would have been likely to have made at the time, a text for the kinds of despair that was being felt during the upheavals and disturbances of the later empire.

What is particularly interesting about it, the quality that distinguishes it from any serious modern counterpart, is its peculiar amalgam of awareness and irrationality, social observation and lugubrious myth or, more accurately, superstition. We may grumble today about the weather having become strangely worse than when we were children and even, in a crackpot vein, believe that the glaciers are swiftly advancing on us or that the air has been irremediably poisoned by atomic fallout or industrial wastes, but we are not likely to think of the earth as having lost its strength or the sun its power to cause growth. (The expected demise of the sun, eons hence, gives no cause for present alarm.) Whatever damage to the physical universe we may see, we interpret it not as a fatality from on high, but, most likely, as the result of stupid, selfish, and short-sighted practices on the part of mankind; in other words, we locate the malady within human will and responsibility.

It seems clear that this conviction or acceptance of decline arose from that still persistent analogy—whether consciously drawn or not—between the body's destiny and that of societies and institutions. Early in the Christian era the Romans articulated such a notion, as Ramsay MacMullen tells us in *Enemies of the Roman Order*. Roman history was made up of "childhood under the ancient kings; youth during the conquest of Italy; maturity during the expansion overseas; and a long, long old age verging to the grave."

Later, in the year 410, during the moment when Rome, already seeming to fail in internal confidence and coherence, was suffering the incursions of Alaric and his Goths, St.

Augustine wrote in a pastoral letter: "Does it surprise you that the world is failing? You are surprised that the world grows old. Man is born, grows up, ages." And, he might have added, dies.

Behind the lack of distinctions in passages such as those of Lucretius and St. Cyprian lies this sovereign power of the body to suggest larger fates than its own. *Everything* marches toward the tomb; nothing is preserved from dissolution. Instead of seeing what we might call "technical" and therefore potentially remediable causes of social and material decline —a misshapen institution, a wrongly conceived political or economic policy—or locating them within the larger sphere of human will or even in historical accident, the ancient world clung to a belief in the inevitability of decay. One result of this was that even where the afflicted institution or activity was clearly the work of men who could be held responsible for it, no principle other than the operation of fatality could be discerned that would account for an apparent fall, a loss of efficiency or vigor.

So customarily keen an observer as Cicero could write with the following blend of fatalism and nostalgia:

Before our time the customs of our people produced outstanding individuals, and ancient customs and traditional institutions were preserved by eminent personalities. In our age, however, the state has come to be like a painting which is remarkable but already fading because of old age, and people neglect not only to restore the original colors in it, but even to preserve its shape and outline.

This image of the state as a "painting," a reality accomplished once and for all but now being slowly eroded, is revealing of how Rome and the entire ancient world tended

[43]

to think of its past. There are affinities with our own awareness of our national history, yet there's a crucial difference
too. We may in America freeze the past in a series of tableaux
—Washington at Valley Forge, Lincoln in his box at Ford's
Theater, the doughboys at Château-Thierry, and so on—but
we would not think of comparing the past itself to a painting,
something that has been rendered all at once and remains
fixed. For us the state, the large formal outcome of past
events on our shores, is continuous, a ceaseless accretion of
ideas, gestures, energies, and impulses, with their incarnation
in behavior and institutions. We may indeed yearn for a time
when the state was better, but it would be difficult for us to
imagine a moment when it was "finished."

Cicero's failure even to attempt an explanation for the disappearance of outstanding individuals and notable personalities, his implicit acceptance of the proposition that "they
don't make them like that any more," is especially useful to
this inquiry for the point it makes that such heroes and
leaders preserved custom and tradition. For it would seem
that to the extent that Greek and Roman thinkers were able
to separate the phenomena of social and cultural decline from
what they saw of the process of decay in the physical universe
itself, they regarded this decline as the result of a kind of
betrayal of the past, a failure to sustain the hard-won victories
over chaos and barbarism that had been gained by a people's
ancestors.

In his celebrated study *Paideia: The Ideals of Greek Culture,* Werner Jaeger remarks that for the Greeks "the supreme
assumption of all education is that moral standards are un-
changeable and that the state institutions designed to produce
a good tradition are permanent." Behind the formally neutral

tone of this observation one senses a world of turbulence and threat; to one area of Greek consciousness any change in moral values and behavior or in the structure of public life meant an opening to the irrational, the ungovernable. It meant that the wall that had been so painstakingly erected against darkness and the unknown, a fragile barrier at best, would collapse under the blows of the unforeseen, the not yet prepared for.

The Greek present can be said to have been held together, then, not so much by what we think of as a confident rationality as by a transmitted faith and what Jaeger calls an "unchanging ideal." It was the gradual loss of this faith, through that questioning of tradition and the gods—for which Euripides, to cite one notable example, was taken to task after his death by Aristotle—and the abandonment of the overriding ideal that were seen to be both the symptoms and the chief causes of decadence (although, as I have said, the word was not used). In *The Republic* Plato outlined the process of degeneration. The son revolts against the father, he says, and goes to the opposite extreme in ever-widening oscillations. Moreover, this insurrection of the son becomes in time a rebellion for its own sake, which is to say a purely formal act, a pose. This is the first expression of what will later be taken to be a profound characteristic of decadence as a cultural condition: a quality of sham passion, of theatrical gesture.

The Romans appeared to have followed the Greek example in locating the source of decadence in this abandonment of or rebellion against the virtues bequeathed by their ancestors. Such virtues, chief among which and holding everything together were those of *nos maiorum,* the ancestral way of life, and *pietas*—a word which meant then essentially what our "piety" does now—undoubtedly had come into being as the result of a long process of moral trial and error, of many imaginative thrusts into the mysteries and obduracies of the spirit and of gross or subtle accommodations to the realities of power.

Yet as history accumulated, generation succeeded generation in that unbroken way which makes it difficult even for us, with our wealth of records, documents, and accumulated testimony of all kinds, to determine where something so impalpable as a public virtue begins (and to the Greeks and Romans all virtue was public). In the classical world the range of material open to the professional historian's or chronicler's inquiry was not supposed to exceed the limits of his own life; everything earlier was considered outside his competence.

And so with their origins shrouded in darkness and even their quite recent pasts in shadow, it must surely have been impossible for ancient societies to trace any clear line of development in moral areas. It must have seemed to the peoples of classical civilizations as if their ancestors, transfigured by the light of the very virtue they had passed on, the binding one of *pietas,* had come upon this supreme value all at once, in a blinding and heroically undertaken transaction with the Sources.

In the absence of detailed recorded history, of what we might call the past as factual communication, the ancient world largely gave over to myth and legend the function that we have assigned to formal historical studies. The problems inherent in this are obvious; what is not so evident is that the mythical apprehension of the origin and destiny of values had the effect of endowing them with immeasurably greater imaginative force than our own "scientific" grasp of such matters is able to give us. What is also true is that to know as much as we do, or think we do, about how values originate is, in an age of deepening irreligion, to tend to make them all equally suspect as spiritual and behavioral imperatives.

Still, the inability of Plato, and the Greek and Roman thinkers who preceded and followed him, to offer any rational explanation for the corruption of traditional values led to a frustration and ill temper on their part such as no other type of problem seems to have caused. It was, after all, the primary problem; if society could not maintain its values, what would become of it?

The difficulty in reasoning the matter through was due in large part to a lack of information, and then to an inability to see process in moral or psychic events. The notion of a rebellion of the young, for instance, makes some sense, but why should it have come about? If the virtues by which a society organizes and guides itself are permanent, how can change insinuate itself into the body politic or suddenly appear like a monster in the streets? If one's ancestors had achieved definitive virtue, what had been the moral state of *their* ancestors, at what point had the fullness been reached?

In their agitated reflections on these questions one can detect a strong note of moralism—that attitude which arises from desperation in the face of a gap between ethical abstractions and imperatives on the one hand and concrete reality on the other. Many fell into a baffled, sullen stance against the unfathomable and seemingly mocking presence of the new. Such a response to changing moral and cultural ways has been in evidence throughout history, of course; our own "counter-culture" and its often distraught critics are a recent case in point. Yet we at least pretend to a more or less scientific understanding of such matters and possess (the more intellectually liberated among us, at any rate) a rooted if sometimes grudging acceptance of change as a law of existence.

In their own efforts at understanding, classical thinkers hit upon two roughly opposed and often self-contradictory types of pseudo-explanation, which have persisted, usually in debased form, into our own time. In their broadest outlines, these were the notions of causation from the outside and from within. The theory of external sources of infection was especially in favor among the Romans, whose vast empire, with its centripetal movement toward the capital city, was rich in possibilities of contamination by alien values and mores.

The portrayals of Greeks in Roman comedy shed an important light on one strand of Roman thinking about the relationship between morality and foreignness. In these plays Greeks were almost always depicted as members of an evil or at best perverse race, and this served as an acceptable cover for satiric portraiture of Rome's own malfeasances. The idea was that an alien, conquered civilization was most likely to have indulged in all the vices, its downfall being precisely the proof of its viciousness, and hence its inferiority.

The more exotic the society or region, the more virulent was likely to be the strain of infection it passed on. Thus the contact of Roman troops with the peoples of Africa and the Near East, together with the presence in Roman households of slaves from those areas, was thought to have introduced into the city cults of strange and debilitating passions and pleasures—in food, dress, sexual practices—whose effect was to replace the "masculine" virtues, particularly those of martial valor and prowess, with soft, sensually indulgent "feminine" behavior and ideals.

Among the last and most subtle of these feminizing influences from the East was of course Christianity, with its emphasis on passivity and resignation in worldly matters and, above all, with its doctrine of the remission of sins. For if sins could be wiped out by a ritual formula of forgiveness, it was argued, then the temptation was there to commit them again and again, a criticism of the Church's moral system that has continued to this day. And so while Christianity preached austerity it simultaneously seemed to introduce a new rationale for hedonism. More fundamentally, the new faith had begun to topple the old gods and so had broken the great chain of piety, a change that helped to leave Rome open to what we have been taught to see as the regressive force of the barbarians.

Overlapping at certain points with the foregoing ideas, the theory of internal causation located the origins of social decline in a general failure of will. In Plato's terms, this meant that the father came in time to lack the conviction necessary to instill in his son his own presumptive reverence for the traditional virtues; at the same time the son came to lack the conviction and filial trust necessary to accept and uphold them.

The causes of this collapse of volition were much debated, but it seems generally to have been ascribed to the habits of luxury and self-indulgence brought about by times of prosperity and most directly by the protracted absence of war.

Long periods of relative peace, such as the Periclean and Augustan ages, resulted, it was said, in a communal *taedium vitae*. In one of his attacks on the spiritual state of Rome, St. Augustine argued, as the historian F. W. Wallbank writes, that "since the destruction of Carthage, her last serious rival, in 146 B.C., her ancient virtues had declined, and the State had been reft asunder by civil discord." Lacking a unifying "cause," a pressure toward the publicly imperative, the people saw their moral energy being sapped and their rulers, on whom they depended for exemplary movements and stances, tempted toward self-gratification in the absence of occasions for risk-taking in the service of the embattled state.

Outside the moral sphere, if we can make a distinction classical thinkers were not given to, decadence was seen to show itself—in agriculture, for example, or the rudimentary manufacturing of the time—as a gradual and inexplicable loss of skills. We know now that both the Greeks and Romans lacked technology in all but the crudest sense and thus possessed almost no repeatable or continuing principle of material creation. They were therefore vulnerable—as many of the world's people are to this day—to the vicissitudes of nature, to extremes of weather, say, or to those demographic cataclysms—such as the uprooting of populations by war or an abrupt decline in the birth rate—which in time can radically affect a society's relation to the physical world and to other peoples.

In this regard, something has come to light recently of crucial importance to an understanding of the ways in which ancient societies struggled to maintain their existence and of the pessimism that marks so much of that exertion. Historians have always been aware that plagues and pestilences have played a major role in human ecology, but not until William H. McNeill's *Plagues and Peoples* was published in 1976 was the full extent of their devastations recognized.

Among the great plagues McNeill discusses was one that struck the Roman Empire in A.D. 165. Impossible to identify, although it may have been smallpox, the disease was epidemic for at least fifteen years and resulted in a death toll that reached in certain places up to a third of the population. The effect, McNeill says, was "a process of continued decay of the population of Mediterranean lands that lasted, despite some local recoveries, for more than half a millennium." A less palpable result, he goes on to say, was that the horror of this epidemic played a significant part in the growing attractiveness of Christianity to the Romans, and their eventual conversion: unlike Christianity, with its doctrine of personal redemption and eternal life, Stoic and other systems of pagan philosophy, whose emphasis was on impersonal process and natural law, were ineffectual in explaining the apparent randomness with which death descended.

Against the catastrophic reality of pestilences and other natural horrors, conventional piety was clearly not going to prevail. But even in the absence of disaster a slow movement of erosion went on. The passing on of skills, which can be thought of as one physical manifestation of the spirit of reverence for and faithfulness to the past, was subject to the tendency of conservative processes to harden into blind mechanical activity, bereft of a full understanding of logical method, in the same way that inherited spiritual values tend fatally to congeal into dogma. The complex reasons for these things are beyond the scope of this book, but that they take place is central to any understanding of what "decadence" might really mean.

The great ironic fact is that, in wishing to preserve what had been valued, classical societies in time found themselves valuing what had been preserved. The result was that, increasingly, value itself became the exclusive province of the past and the present was transformed into something resembling a vast association of museums: a Smithsonian Institution of artifacts, physical procedures, mechanisms, a Louvre of consciousness and received imagination. The "crisis" of the ancient world, so much talked about and fretted over in later historiography, can be seen to have lain most fundamentally in this steady accumulation of the past within all the spaces of the present, so that to live must have in time become to *have been lived,* to be the abode of ghosts. This fate is perennial, in some degree; we have Ibsen's play to remind us of its "modern" operation. But it must in ancient times have been universal, profound, wholly inescapable.

Ramsay MacMullen writes: "A child was born into a praenomen, a nomen and a cognomen, all parts of which committed him to the character of earlier namesakes—to whom, as he grew up, he offered sacrifices in his home, and for whose deeds he was ridiculed or respected by his friends as son (or grandson, or great-grandson) of the man who did thus-and-so."

MacMullen goes on to describe a typical funeral of a powerful or upper-class Roman:

At [the start of the ceremonies] an actor who looked and talked most like him [the dead man] or perhaps some relative who resembled him, put on his death mask of wax, exactly painted, and walked ahead of his bier, accompanied by dozens or (for a great man of a great family) by hundreds of his ancestors represented in turn by their masks and by the robes and rites of the highest office they had attained, so that the whole procession brought together praetors and consuls, generals and party leaders reaching back through generations.

We are not accustomed to regard the fate of the ancient world in this way, and it may therefore seem presumptuous for a non-historian to offer a perspective of this kind. But history is very far from being an exact science, and laymen have the right to question the way it is practiced. History traditionally, and according to its own conception of its task, properly, has been the record of events (*res gestae,* things done) and not of states of being. Or if the latter, then these are psychic or spiritual situations for which it is believed eventful origins can and ought to be found. We have a need to find physical, material causes for impalpable dénouements. Rome "fell," we have decided, because of certain observable, more or less concrete conditions, which functioned as *causes:* the overextension of physical resources, internal political and social discord, the loss of military élan and cohesion due to the large number of mercenaries and subject peoples in her armies, inferior will and decisiveness in the face of the vitality and untroubled consciences of her enemies. All of this is said to have constituted in the largest sense Rome's decadence.

It scarcely occurs to us that such interpretations explain nothing. They are in fact elements of the cause-and-effect mode of looking at human experience which historians have continually brought over from the physical sciences and which are still being employed to this moment. The rare historian who moves beyond that is the one who apprehends the mysterious nature of human will and imagination, those factors that intervene in the processes of physical actuality and that have perpetually resisted being confined to a realm of predictability, an order of logic and rationally determined truths.

This is not to say that history is unknowable or a matter of pure guesswork, but only that the history of nature apart from man or including man solely in his biological aspects—the sphere of the physical sciences—is of a different order from that which attempts to interpret the sphere he does uniquely occupy. Philosophers have spoken of man as being both within and outside of nature, precariously balanced. It was Georges Bataille who wrote that the difference between biological sex—sex as animals know it—and eroticism is that the former is a given, a mode of existence inexorably and uniformly imposed on every creature, while the latter is a construction, an invention of the human mind and spirit. Eroticism emerges as a partially free act that surpasses nature, subverts it in some ways, and lives as though by a new creation.

In much the same way politics, too, is an invention; society itself is one. This doesn't mean that human beings are perfectly free to devise and live by whatever principles and processes they wish. Far from it. The state of the physical or natural world, and especially of our understanding of it, determines to a great extent what is possible to be "invented" at any moment and during any period, what culture it is possible to have. Fernand Braudel has shown in *The Mediterranean* how geography radically affects civilized endeavors, and it is obvious that a brutally hard material existence, a society living close to the borders of starvation or peculiarly subject to disease, will have little energy or space for the devising of any but minimal structures of the mind. Or a society may be so organized that the vast majority of the populace find their lives consumed in sheer physical labor while a leisured ruling class develops human constructions for the group, its "culture." The choices may be arrived at undemocratically, but they are choices nevertheless.

In a technological society such as ours, where the breathing space after physical toil is capacious, culture tends to be immensely various, full of the most subtle refinements as well as having many grotesque aspects that result from numerous imaginations, of one or another degree of coherence, being free to roam everywhere. Still, the point is that culture, the dimension of values, desires, hopes, fears, and consciousness beyond the biological, is always a matter of choices, not laws, at the very least of choice asserting itself at some point beyond the iron suzerainty of the Law.

I have been leading up to what will doubtless appear to be the very strange notion that decline or decadence was in a certain manner an invention of the ancient world, a choice of belief, however coerced by experience the choice seemed to be and however narrow the area in which it was made. The first thing to say about this is that choice, as I have been defining it, implies the possibility of error, of making mistakes, being wrong. Cultures are full of such "mistakes": bad art, erroneous philosophies, wrongly conceived scientific procedures, suffocating moral systems, and so on. Yet to be in error is still to live by human decisions, to be more than the vassal of nature inexorably bound by its laws or truths. There are no mistakes in nature; even freaks reflect the Law.

The history of human consciousness might be thought of, in part, as a struggle, through error, toward an equality with nature, or at least what is posited as the "natural," in the realm of truth. Science can certainly be regarded in this way. Needless to say, what is done in the presence of physical truth (whether to use nuclear technology for bombs or for peaceful energy is a gross example) brings us into a moral dimension, one of choice, where new "errors" perpetually thrust themselves forward to be made, and where human distinctiveness therefore continues to display itself.

The "mistake" of the classical world in regard to decadence arose from many sources, chief among them the veneration for the past I have been speaking of. The choice involved in this was constrained on every side, but it remained a choice, an act of the mind and will; the observable world did not contain the action or principle of decadence as it does avalanches, tidal waves, or, closer to the point, the phenomenon of aging. It seems necessary now to make a foray into an area of metaphysical or philosophical speculation through which alone, I suspect, history can be made to reveal what it ordinarily holds back: not its truths but its lies.

There is no obvious reason why the idea of "progress" should have entered civilized consciousness so much later than that of decline or decadence and why until relatively recently it should have been so much weaker and less influential than they. Without knowing more about decadence than its literal dictionary meaning suggests, one would expect it to be a condition and hence a consideration primarily of old and tired societies. Progress, it goes without saying, is a concept of time to come, and what more expansive future could there ever have been than that which lay like the most boundless of seas in front of the earliest civilizations or later classical ones in their beginnings? Yet we know of Hesiod's despair and of how Roman writers so early found the present wanting by comparison with the past and the future a source of dread.

To begin to resolve this apparent paradox, it might be useful to reflect on a curious discussion that took place at various times during the Middle Ages, an argument having to do with the nature of time in relation to history. Medieval scholars found themselves debating whether their societies ought to be regarded as old, inasmuch as they had come into being after all previous societies, or young, in the sense that they were new, "children" of their ancestors and of the entire past. In the same way it was wondered whether ancient civilizations, especially the familiar and centrally important ones of Greece and Rome, ought to be thought of as old, which is how one would naturally regard them from the perspective of the present, or young, the standpoint from which it must be supposed they naturally would have considered themselves.

This debate is likely to strike most of us as the epitome of scholastic reasoning, yet it contains a clue to the problem of social and cultural "decline," the problem, that is to say, not of its historical causes but, more fundamentally, of how to think about it. To begin with, if the past is "old" from one point of view but "young" from another, then in a certain sense the present must also be. And if this is so, then the present's relationship to both the past and the future becomes far more mysterious and unstable than we have been accustomed to think.

If we consider the matter of social development and possibility, we have to ask ourselves whether or not we who are alive today are not fatally saddled with the past, carrying it around on our collective shoulders; are we not "old" before we start? Or does being "children" of previous societies mean that we are young, collectively, in the sense of having a more or less open future, one that the past obviously influences but does not irresistibly control? This is the way we generally regard our own personal futures when we are physically young but old enough to know what a future is. The tyranny of the past, Ibsen's ghosts in our heads, makes itself known to us only as we get older and are more and more called upon for efficacious choices.

In an age of scientific prowess and technical answers to what were once metaphysical questions, we have collectively become more and more complacent about time, whatever the quality of life in the present. In so far as it affects society and its institutions, we think of time as at least theoretically a progressive movement, however "tragic" our imagination is in regard to personal life. (In fact society's very progress—if it can be said, for example, to have become more and more rational—may be an element in our pessimism.) The most frequent metaphor for this is a river or road carrying us along to increasingly predictable or at any rate imaginable destinations, and containing within itself, like the biblical Jordan, and again theoretically, a principle or agency of remedy. Accepting this vision of time as movement, we are likely to turn a cold shoulder to the past, that reminder of how all portions of time give out and are successively "spent" and so brought to a standstill. For some of us this leads to an active denunciation of the past, as a kind of impertinence, if not a horror, a field, at the very least, of mistakes.

Yet as certain works of art and literature have the power to teach us, time is an actuality that keeps us blind to its real nature, which is neither progressive nor the reverse but simply the *dimension of being.* In *Happy Days,* like all of Samuel Beckett's work a play that deals with time as a "double-headed monster of salvation and damnation," the protagonist is buried first up to her waist and then to her neck in sand, which everything in the text tells us is an objective correlative for time itself. We are *in* time, encased in it like an animal in its pelt, and the only way we can distinguish it as something passing instead of a medium like air or water is to observe the physical changes that take place in the world and in ourselves: the growth of living things, the alternations of seasons, rusting metals, eroding cliffs, graying hair, double chins, most decisively the deaths of creatures and of each other.

But this means that we can know time only in an *ex post facto* way, so to speak, after it has run part of its "course"; we can know it only by its effects. Each of us constitutes, in fact, one of these effects, each is infected from the beginning with a principle, a virus of "oldness." Since we live in a world ruled by death, which is forever overcoming the counter-sovereignty of birth, since species may endure but individuals do not, to be physically new or young is from one perspective to be material for becoming old and so for death. Naturally, we don't walk about under the direct or sustained weight of this knowledge—the very young are like picnickers in the shadow of its gates—but either suppress it as effectively and for as long as we can or convert it into proverbs and adages or, more weightily, into philosophical or religious consciousness. The effect of doing this is to make our awareness of death in a certain manner unreal, one or another form of abstract, "literary" acceptance.

The impersonal and technical counterpart of this process of forgetfulness and consolation is the conversion of the data of mortality into scientific knowledge. In this regard something strange shows itself. The familiar optimism that is supposed to characterize science can be seen to be less a matter of direct power over nature in the present, and so to a degree over the physical future, than one of confidence based on control of the past. To know what has specifically happened in time, to be able physically to unearth time's buried effects and, most important, to have the intellectual tools to make time yield itself up as development, these things make it possible to connect the past to the present in such a way as to make the future seem to beckon as part of an unbroken series.

All this gives us an opening into the reason for the idea of decline being of so much longer standing and of so much greater influence on the human mind throughout history than that of progress. In his well-known study *The Idea of Progress,* J. B. Bury wrote that "the achievements of physical science [in the nineteenth century] did more than anything else to convert the imaginations of men to the general doctrine of progress." It was not until science had begun to offer *predictable* power over the earth, a power based in large part on the observance of continuity in nature, that the future could be seen to be an enticement instead of a threat. Cause and effect: what better formula is there for expressing reliable, unclouded relations between the past and the future?

Where no such relations are felt to exist, the future has little reality as a lure. The past weighs, dictates, occupies the present like a house ruled over by parents who do not die. The present is mostly seen not as the outcome of the past but as its accretion. As archaeologists and historians now know, early civilizations and societies therefore felt themselves much more bound to the sway of the past than later ones, while the most recent of all—think of the new African states —are quite desperately impelled toward the future.

This has very little to do with questions of a society's sickness or health. We see nearly powerless nations attempting to rush headlong into the future precisely because other, older nations, however turbulent or "ill" they may be, seem already to occupy it. For such peoples "progress," conceived almost wholly as technological advance, serves as a most potent myth, in the same way that decline or decadence, as we have seen, functioned as a negative one for societies which, however troubled they might have been, nevertheless regarded themselves as having at some point in their pasts reached the limits of human possibility.

We have been talking about a *sense* of progress and decline. What is needed for a theory of these movements, an intellectual formulation, is, naturally, a conception of time as linear, neutrally so at first. Time has to be conceived of as stretching out ahead and behind like a road or a serial narrative, and not simply as a piling up of minutes, days, and years, as in Zeno's famous image of the heap of millet. In other words, there has to be available that rationalized escape from time as the element we inhabit, a liberation from time as an eternal present. To think in formal ways about progress and decline is, then, to be able to think about chronology, about human life as history. In static civilizations such as the Egyptian or early Mediterranean (whose stasis was, in fact, due to their having succumbed to or willingly accepted the reality of time as motionless) such historical thinking is rudimentary at best, so that clear consciousness of the effects of time is mostly replaced by intuition, quasi-mystical or wholly emotional assessments of reality and possibility.

The condition is of course "prescientific" and thus a realm from which "progress" has a more difficult time emerging than does "decline." For the past, however obscure its rational connection to the present may be, has at least been actual, existing in artifacts and monuments or in memory or the transmitted knowledge of others' memories, while the future, to which progress by definition moves, is entirely unreal. This is difficult for us to imagine, but in the work of at least one great playwright, Chekhov, the proposition becomes actual. In *The Three Sisters,* for example, the future, so much talked about, so desired, cannot be reached; it is denied the characters in order that the only actuality, the present, may be lived in. *The Three Sisters* is a play about what happens while the women *do not get to Moscow,* just as *Waiting for Godot* is a drama about what Didi and Gogo do *while* Godot doesn't come. The point in both cases is that the present is the only reality.

We tend to regard the future as an extension of the present, a coiling road the only visible segment of which is the one we occupy. We may not wish to see what is around the bend, but we implicitly accept that we will come to it, that it will be there. The image misleads us into thinking that the future is real, on reserve, so to speak, biding its time, when the truth—a commonplace in philosophic discussions of time —is that the future is only real, actual, when it has become the present and so, in effect, destroyed itself.

For the ancient world the future seems to have begun as unreality. Impelled nevertheless toward it, this human universe hung back in the familiarity of the past, holding to what had remained of it and ritually mourning what had departed. As the historical sense grew, as history itself accumulated, the expression of regret for the lost past gained in intensity and specificity, while at the same time an idea of progress, or at least a notion that something better might be possible in time, began to make itself known as a countervailing pressure upon pessimism. Yet such "optimism," if that is the word for it, was thin and entirely lacking in detail. The ancient world would have been astonished by a proposal for a scholarly conference on what life is going to be like a hundred years from now, or even ten.

Hope may have been held out for the future, plans may have been drawn up, but in the absence of any true understanding of the dynamics of change, or even of the materials for that guesswork which provides so much activity for social scientists today, the cast of the mind was almost purely wishful. Christianity, of course, contained a strong element of wish or hope; in stern doctrinal terms it required faith in the future, which would redeem the age and all ages. But this was what lifted the new faith out of time and therefore posed so great a threat to the sacred past. As Santo Mazzarino writes in *The End of the Ancient World,* "there is an insoluble contradiction between the classical tradition, which is formally untouchable, and the spiritual revolution, which has already corroded and weakened it."

Outside the new faith, what was real was a sense of loss, of something of the essence of value having lapsed away or been subtly slain. Where to begin to arrest the drift? Where indeed, when there was no real drift at all, but only the fearsome neutrality of time, which demands that the present create itself, with the materials of the past, to be sure, but in no spirit of perpetuating all that has already been. What the ancient world saw as decline was really change seen as loss. Or, it might be, gain seen as loss. Was Christianity an "advance," or a step backward? Nietzsche thought the latter. Gibbon, echoing an earlier observation of Voltaire's, saw the fall of Rome as the "triumph of barbarism *and* [italics added] religion." Yet we generally oppose the two, and it is one of the great contradictions in our theory of Rome's disastrous "end" that Christianity, which our central tradition holds as positive, an accession, should be assigned a role as agent of destruction.

Another contradiction in our perspective on the ancient world, with Rome as the *locus classicus,* is that we see it as obeying an iron law of decline and fall. We are not troubled by the fact that although we think the Romans' fate inevitable we still hold them responsible for it, still search for its causes in their behavior and institutions. There is a parallel here to the Christian doctrine of the inevitability of sin being found together with the culpability of the individual sinner. Yet such tension between freedom and necessity can operate only on a metaphysical or theological level; with regard to that actuality we call Roman history, one has to choose.

Either Rome was the victim of an inexorable process of decay, in which case nothing would have made any difference, or else she brought the calamity down on herself, in which case different behavior or actions could have prevented it. Theories abound concerning what those changed actions might have been; Ortega y Gasset, for example, was one of many who thought that Rome's fate might have been averted had she been able to replace the structures of the old state with new forms of representative democracy. The source of "decadence," then, is in this failure.

But what in fact was Rome's fate? We are accustomed to thinking that she "fell" and that this fall was essentially the result of an internal failure to which the onslaught of the barbarians merely added the *coup de grâce*. And we have decided that "decadence" is the suitable word to describe a malady that had several manifestations: the indifference of the mighty to the proper exercise of power, their pursuit of pleasure at the cost of vigorous rule, the erosion of political energy in the general society, the sapping and eventual disappearance of an ongoing sense of responsibility and, with that, of any faith in the straightforward, the "workable," and the resolute in human affairs.

But before we look into the question of whether in fact Rome fell and what that might mean if it were so, it has to be understood, everything suggests, that whatever happened, decadence, as we have been used to conceiving of it, had nothing to do with it. Most obvious in this regard, the fourth century was one of the more coherent and unperverse eras of Roman moral history. As Jerome Buckley writes in *The Triumph of Time,* "if lasciviousness were the chief cause of decline, Rome would have perished centuries before the barbarians swooped down upon the Christian and relatively moral community." And the fact was also that the period from Augustus to Commodus, the era of Rome's greatest military power and most vigorous political condition, was precisely that of her citizens' most flamboyant and perverse sexual and sensual behavior.

The historian André Piganiol has written:

It is a mistake to say that Rome was decadent. Plundered and disfigured by the barbarian invaders of the third century, it rose again from the ruins. At the same time and at the cost of a great crisis it carried through a labor of internal transformation. A new conception of Imperial power was formed, the Byzantine; a new conception of truth and beauty, the medieval; a new conception of collective and joint work in the service of society . . . Roman civilization did not die a natural death. It was murdered.

Historians have come around only slowly to this truth, and many still deny it. For it upsets too many theories and, more fundamentally, goes against our habit of fitting experience into logical patterns. The interrelatedness of historical facticity—in so far as historians presumably determine it—and systems of value are deep and complex, but one thing we can say is that historical facts are never able to speak for themselves in even the limited but poignant way a contemporary fact can, through its *presence,* its sheerly being there before us. The past has no voice of its own, only ours in its mouth.

In the case of Rome the "facts" have been bent into theory, inserted into a system of judgment designed for (or at any rate having the effect of) bolstering our belief in historical process as essentially logical and determinable. Roman civilization, as defined by the maintenance of the imperial power in the city itself, and by the control of the city-state over its own political and cultural destiny, did not expire through the operation of some principle of decay, eternal and inexorable or not. It did not die as a body normally does, slumping toward the grave. Matters over which it had no control—the existence of other societies and peoples who possessed physical force, without the vision of order and structure that redeemed Rome from all its excesses; the envy and rapacity of the human world outside—brought about its "death."

The analogy to the human body moving from the cradle to the tomb does not hold. There is nothing inevitable about the loss of power in civilizations; people age and institutions do, but not societies, since these are forever being renewed on the simple biological level, so that it is merely a figure of speech to talk of "age" and "youth" in this regard. As Rémy de Gourmont wrote with such keen insight: "The long decadence of expiring empires is one of the most remarkable illusions of history. If certain empires died of sickness or old age, the majority of them, on the contrary, perished a violent death, in the plenitude of their physical power, in the full force of their intellectual vigor."

Dying Rome intellectually vigorous? The argument persists that the inferiority of late Roman art and poetry is evidence of decadence, at least in the cultural sphere. But were that poetry and art in fact inferior? Once again our censure is self-contradictory. We accuse late Roman poetry of decadence for being "formalist," imitative, and late Roman art for being rough, untutored, bizarre. Decadence thus catches in its net that which fails because it repeats the past and that which does so because it veers away from it or falls beneath it. In both cases what lies behind the judgment is an ideal, a completed and sanctified notion of beauty. "It is the corollary of this conception of a model performance," the art historian E. H. Gombrich has said, "that once the problem has been mastered the only alternatives are imitation or decline."

If we consider late Roman art inferior it is usually because we assume that her artists had somehow declined in skill and taken on perverse attitudes toward the proper subject of art; the truth is that they had altered intentions, new subjects for which different skills were required. In *The End of the Ancient World,* Santo Mazzarino writes: "We now recognize a stylistic sensibility in late Roman art as lively as any other and also quite new and revealing: 'the representation,' said Alois Riegl [a German art historian], 'of the individual form in infinite space' . . . Decadence 'does not exist.' " Mazzarino goes on to say that "lovers of pure form and of rational perspective will of course continue to prefer classical to late Roman art"—this is the heart of the matter.

For if decadence is a falling away or down, this movement has to be carried on in relation to standards, norms, "classic" achievements from which any departure would necessarily be considered a defection, an evil. This is how the ancient world saw it and how we, much less consciously, see it now. One begins to suspect that whatever decadence may be it plays a scapegoat role as a word, an ascription. And it serves, it seems, to cover up our ignorance of, or refusal to see, how the world operates in one of its deepest dimensions independently of what we call cause and effect.

In order to account for the barbarian conquest of Rome, the latter's decadence is cited as a truism. But the barbarians were simply *there,* powerful, ruthless, provoked into action not by Rome's decadence but by her presence, Rome that had tried to do too much. Our view of the event is a construct, a tale. Decadence is posited in the light of an ideal fiction—Rome in the fullness of its vigor, its *image* of vigor. When Rome changed, when she moved toward Christianity, for example, the ideal was betrayed.

The very success of Rome led not to her fall but to the *idea* of that fall, the notion of a great muscular organism being secretly eaten by a cancer. But the truth is that when on the political level Rome collapsed, great strains of energy were passed on, the world after Rome was shaped and inspirited by her having existed. History is not a chronicle of discrete events or epochs, nor is it to be understood in categorical ways. Everything connects. The reason "decadence" will not do as a description of Rome is that it does injustice to both her past and her future; she did not wind down, she did not disappear, nor did she bring down on herself her own fate. Fate was there, and fate is another word for change.

3

UNTIL A LITTLE OVER A CENTURY AGO, AS
far as we can determine, no person had ever been described
as "decadent," much less as *a* decadent, the way we might
speak of someone as a puritan, a pervert, or, in a less condemnatory type of judgment, a romantic. *Things* were said
to be decadent, conditions, states of public and communal
existence, but neither the adjective nor the noun had been
attached to particular human beings. In addition to this, for
several hundred years before the word crossed the gap between social abstraction and human specificity the idea it
pointed to had to undergo a process of disentanglement from
superstition, from quasi-mystical acceptance as the inevitable
fate of civilizations.

What we might call the "modern" concept of social decadence seems to have begun to take shape during the early
decades of the sixteenth century, at first in Italy. In the
medieval period the classical notion of decline (to use a
neutral term more in keeping with linguistic practice of the
time) as a mysterious phenomenon, but one within the order
of nature, had given way to a view of it as being part of a
divine plan: if the world was "running down," it was in
preparation for its eventual resurrection in eternity. But in
the sixteenth century this sense of a fatefulness in which all
things were swallowed up began gradually to be replaced by
a more or less rational consideration of social, political, and,
eventually, cultural and personal actuality.

In Italy this sense of decline stemmed at first from what
must have appeared to have been solid evidence: the patent

decay of republican institutions as the city-states lost their verve and their markets, the plague of foreign invasions and domination. Elsewhere the "evidence" was different. As consciousness of secular responsibility for human destiny spread through Europe, scrutiny began to shift from institutions to individual behavior. A Spanish satirist, Francisco de Quevedo, could be found arguing, for example, that his countrymen had been infected with *"decadencia"* by their traffic with alien and presumably inferior peoples; they had learned habits of excessive eating and drinking from the Germans, unnatural sexual practices from the Italians, and so on. Although this ascription resembled one element of Roman thinking about the subject, it was no longer tinged with any deep sense of fatality, as had been the case in classical times.

It was in France that decadence early became a central issue and there that it was given the most agitated attention. The first recorded "scientific" work of any length on the subject was an elaborate treatise on political decline, full of conventional notions about corrupt institutions and the like, by one Claude Duret, who in 1595 published his *Discours de la vérité des causes et effets des décadences . . . et ruines des monarchies, empires . . . et républiques.* By the end of the seventeenth century in France the literal meaning of the word "decadence" as a "falling away" or "down" had become obsolete, though that significance hung at the back of most future usage; at the same time the term itself had driven from currency its erstwhile rivals, *déclinaison* and *inclinaison.* These were words that came directly from classical Latin and reflected Roman preoccupation with social retrogression as a mysterious leaning or slippage. "Decadence" also took on at this time an implication of moral corruption and irresponsibility it had previously only vaguely and erratically possessed. By the middle of the eighteenth century French thinkers were widely convinced of their country's inexorable decline and were eagerly searching in both private and public areas for rational explanations of the process.

In *The Sense of Decadence in Nineteenth Century France,* Konrad Swart tells of a letter Voltaire wrote from Fermi in 1770 to his friend LaHarpe, in which he offered the following bit of advice: "Don't hope to re-establish good taste; we are in a time of the most horrible decadence." Somewhat earlier Montesquieu had given as his opinion that France's dwindling population (the evidence for which must surely have been rather shaky) was a sign and a proof of her decadence, as such a thing had been for ancient civilizations, and he had gone on to deplore the "enervating" effects of his countrymen's habits of luxury. A hundred years later, Proudhon would speak of decadence as "moving at an accelerated pace: conscience, intelligence, character, all perish within it."

What would these writers have thought of the following characteristically grand and perverse dictum of the Marquis de Sade's: "The happiest state will always be that in which depravity of manners and morals is most universal"? Or this sentiment of Flaubert's: "I love above all the sight of vegetation resting upon old ruins; this embrace of nature coming swiftly to bury the work of man the moment his hand is no longer there to defend it, fills me with deep joy"? Or more astonishing still, of the founding in 1886 of a literary and cultural journal called *Le Décadent,* whose editor, a minor poet and aesthete named Anatole Baju, declared in the first issue that a new human type had arisen, the decadent, whose representatives were the "precursor(s) of the society of the future"? The decadent, Baju went on to say, was "a man of progress . . . painstaking . . . economical, hard-working and straight in all his habits . . . simple . . . correct . . . the master of his senses . . . calm, serene . . . [with] the virtue of a stoic."

It was between these antipodal attitudes and assertions of meaning that "decadence" as a notion and a piece of language took its exceedingly queer course in eighteenth- and nineteenth-century France. The strangeness is as much verbal as intellectual; the destiny is of a word no less than of an idea. For when we have run through all the possible dichotomies around which we organize so many of our efforts at historical understanding—rational versus irrational modes of consciousness; optimistic versus pessimistic theories of politics and human nature; classic versus romantic dispositions, and the like—we are left with the awareness that no such polarizations of thinking are of much use in this case.

For what can we make of the conversion, on the part of some minds at least, of a pejorative into an honorific and, beyond the purely linguistic, of the embrace of what had always been regarded with sorrow or detestation? Something new had entered the intellectual and moral atmosphere in which "decadence" exhibited itself and was announced, so that a traditional idea could have been turned into its opposite. This period in France, especially from around 1850 to the end of the century, was the historical epoch in which debate about the nature and reality of decadence was most intense and widespread, but at the same time when the word's accepted meanings and usages were most flagrantly contradictory, most opaque, and most "unhistorical."

To begin to understand the events of this era as they concerned the idea of decadence, we have to consider for a moment the status of what we can think of as an apparently opposing idea, that of "progress." As we noted earlier, progress is a late belief or hypothesis or, if one prefers, illusion. It could take full hold in the mind only after science and technology had begun to establish human control over the physical world through the ability to predict the operations of nature and to repeat, without a continual process of trial and error, the necessary steps in productive labor of all kinds. In its most fundamental or material sense, Progress is the intellectual legatee of the industrial revolution. Aflame with optimism, the *Edinburgh Review* apotheosized the great London Exhibition of 1851, with its display of machinery and technical wonders, as the unrolling of "the living scroll of human progress, inscribed with every successive conquest of man's intellect."

The moral expression of this confidence in material and scientific advance lay in what we have come to think of as bourgeois smugness and complacency; the philosophical expression or attitude was a sense of the future as alluring, with the physical past already disarmed and overcome; the artistic expression was the Academy. Against this set of peculiarly linked strands of optimism and conservative practice there came into being a movement of disaffiliation and rejection; a critique took shape of both the optimists and the idea of progress itself. The main lines of this chapter of intellectual history are thoroughly familiar; in France, where the chief battles were fought, the most vivid formulation of what occurred is perhaps that of bohemian versus bourgeois (to borrow the title of a useful book by César Grana). What is not so well known is the manner in which the repudiated optimism and self-satisfaction were replaced by what we can only call an apocalyptic negativity, an aggressive despair.

In the roughest of divisions, disaffection with the quality and direction of life in France from, say, 1820 on fell into two main categories. The lines were fluid and many of the dissidents spent time in both camps, but we can speak with some accuracy of two groups: a party of optimists (though scarcely so in the bourgeois sense that has been described) and one composed of people of a more literary or artistic bent who lacked political interest and hope. The former, loosely, were the adherents of what has come to be called Social Romanticism, whose intellectual forefather, if such things can ever be so precisely determined, was Rousseau, with Diderot and the other great figures of the Enlightenment also exerting various degrees of influence. It was the social romantics, convinced of the possibility of communal regeneration, who were in the forefront of political agitation, and it was they, naturally, who felt most deeply betrayed and disoriented by the aftermath of the upheavals of 1848.

If the optimists represented the social and political aspects of the Romantic movement, the pessimists were the inheritors of its personal and imaginative ones. Though a writer or artist in the early decades of the century might for a time combine the two impulses, increasingly to be in literature or the other arts meant an abandonment of political belief and fervor. Flaubert, with his profound disillusionment after 1848, was only one notable case of this flight. As the century went on, hope of a revivifying change became more and more a matter for the private self. Gérard de Nerval described the shifting, unstable, but increasingly individualistic and apolitical atmosphere in which people of sensibility lived:

Our period was a mixture of activity, hesitation and idleness; of brilliant Utopias, philosophical or religious aspirations, vague enthusiasms . . . boredom, discord and uncertain hopes. Ambition was not of our age . . . and the greedy race for position and honors drove us away from spheres of political activity. There remained to us only the poet's ivory tower where we mounted ever higher to isolate ourselves from the crowd. In those high altitudes we breathed at last the pure air of solitude; we drank forgetfulness in the golden cup of legend; we were drunk with poetry and love.

Some time before de Nerval composed this apologia and manifesto, Goethe had offered to Eckermann the following estimate of the new writers in France: "They begin to declare tedious the representations of noble sentiments and deeds and attempt to treat of all sorts of abominations. Instead of the beautiful subjects from Grecian mythology, there are devils, witches and vampires, and the lofy heroes of antiquity must give place to jugglers and galley slaves." Goethe was referring most pointedly to Victor Hugo, but, as the author of the dictum that the classic in art was the healthy and the romantic the diseased, he might have traced the "malady" further back to its sources in the previous era, when the French Revolution had begun to undermine classical values, in art as in so many other realms.

Literary genealogies are the most problematic of constructions, but we certainly can say that behind the dark or "abominable" side of French Romanticism stood, to begin with, Chateaubriand. Mario Praz has called Chateaubriand the "forerunner of the Decadence," the term that would come to be applied formally to the cultural climate and movement that held sway for a time in the last decades of the nineteeth century and of which *Le Décadent* was a brief quasi-official voice. Chateaubriand's imagination, according to Praz, was quintessentially decadent (like so many other writers on the subject, Praz has complete confidence that he knows what the word means) in its combination of an "epicurean" Catholicism with a streak of sexual cruelty, and in its perverse taste for what Chateaubriand himself called "melancholy landscapes." The first trait or disposition anticipates Joris-Karl Huysmans and the last one Baudelaire and Flaubert, as well as, among many others, the painter Puvis de Chavannes. In a letter of 1861 Puvis confessed to a friend that he had a weakness for "mournful" aspects of nature and insisted that "bad weather has more life than good."

This last remark is an especially revealing clue to the entire change in sensibility that was to result, after Romanticism had faded as a position or cult, in the so-called Decadent spiritual program and style, and it points to an ancestor even more profoundly generative and directly exemplary than Chateaubriand: Sade. When Durtal, in Huysmans' novel about Satanism, *Là Bas* (*Down There*), says that "one can take pride in going as far in crime as in virtue," he is of course echoing a central notion of Sade; when Baudelaire, earlier, asserts that it is "always necessary to return to Sade, that is to say to the *natural* man [italics added] in order to explain evil" he is delineating the ground from which Sade's influence rose; and he is at the same time, as we shall see, exposing as myth the notion of the Decadent movement as being simply a perverse love of evil and a willful cultivation of corrupt eccentricity, an idea that remains largely in force in our own day.

Sade, a cultural progenitor in many ways, was supremely so in one: as the consciousness which, in one sphere of the mind if not in action, refused to be bound by established values, inherited and institutionalized pieties. In ascribing to him a status as "natural," Baudelaire identified his chief exemplary power. In so far as any individual thinker can be, Sade was the originator or, more accurately, the first compelling enunciator in modern times of the desire to be other than what society determined, to act otherwise than existing moral structures coerced one into doing. And Sade was surely a type of thinker; his most grotesque sexual fantasies were at bottom ideas about behavior, about appetite and human predicaments.

At some level the hunger was no doubt for an impossible freedom, and this ache for what will not be permitted both by the circumscriptions of the self and by the limits of social being is of course a romantic characteristic, one that will make itself known again in the Decadent period. Still, in having had his furious dreams, Sade was a benefactor. One of his greatest bequests to those who came after him, a gift of a similar order to the one Marx bestowed, was the recognition of the debt morality owes to power, the ways in which values of all kinds are shaped and held in place by material forces.

The chief power of the age was that of industrialism, and the chief value which industrialism set in motion and upheld was that of productivity. It was Stendhal, surely with a clue from Sade, who first observed that the enlistment of human energy in the service of ever-increasing productivity, and the consequent necessity to organize society in ever more complex and rationalized ways, could be accomplished only at the expense of the affective life. This perception throws clear light on the origin of the aesthetic reaction to bourgeois hegemony, as well as on *l'art pour l'art,* bohemianism, and, as it will turn out, on decadence as a formal position or value.

Baudelaire spoke of the good bourgeois as "an enemy of art, of perfume, a fanatic of utensils." By this invective he was defending the nonutilitarian in an age that seemed to worship only the immediately useful. (Utility, Nietzsche said later, is simply another heresy by which we live, and by which we may some day die.) Similarly, when Théophile Gautier argued that art expressed only itself—one of the earliest statements of the aesthetic as an independent value— he was attempting to disengage it from its uses as bourgeois expression. Art, that is to say, is no mere embellishment to practical life, as in the employment of received notions of beauty in the service of communal aggrandizement or consolation, nor is it the servant of power. It is instead its critic or alternative.

If progress was thus tied to utilitarianism, moral advance no less than material, it is understandable that art, the preeminently impractical human activity, should have become the banner under which the opponents of the age would group themselves. "The idea of progress," Baudelaire wrote, "that ridiculous idea that flourishes on the soil of modern fatuity." Ernest Renan, no zealot of the aesthetic in Baudelaire's terms but a humanist of wide sympathies, was enunciating a conviction held most passionately by artists, writers, and moral thinkers when he declared in the 1840s, at the beginning of his career, that "our century is not moving toward either good or evil; it is moving toward mediocrity." It is not surprising, then, that Frédéric Ozanam, the French Catholic historian and ardent democrat, could assert in 1852 that "progress" had become a discredited notion, but it is surely unsettling that he should have gone on to say that in place of progress the best minds of his generation now believed, in one way or another, in decadence.

What could this mean? How was it possible to *believe* in something historically so negative and destructive of human substance, the very principle, it would seem, of exhaustion and loss? The best minds of the time, it was clear, did not simply accept the fact of decadence but had begun, strangely, to have faith in it, the way one might in a religion, say, or astrology, or, for that matter, progress. But how was it possible to celebrate the decline of things? In our own era Paul Éluard might seem to have put the question in a more detailed and lyrical way when he asked about Baudelaire, "why did he make it his business to carry on an uncompromising struggle against healthy reality . . . why did he oppose evil in the making to ready-made good, the devil to God . . . clouds to clear and motionless skies?"

Fatuity, mediocrity, ready-made good—these are the epithets that put us in the way of understanding. Whatever the perversity of individual minds, however often (as is true in all periods) boredom became an excuse for corrupt sensuality, the cumulative testimony of the era's keenest minds was to its commonplaceness, the insipidity of its most triumphant enterprises, the dullness that emanated from its "health." As an aspect of all this, the spreading democratization of society brought alarm to the artistic mind. "Faced with the advent of the democratic public," César Grana writes in his study of French bohemianism, "and the opening of society to democratic impulses, men of letters reacted by returning intellectual acts to a mythical atmosphere." In a movement with affinities to aspects of our arts today, they also returned intellectual acts to a hieratic and jealously personal ambiance, and did it all in the name of a new or revived aristocracy of utterance and gesture, intending by it a grave, passionate rebuke to the philistines.

In 1845 the novelist and essayist Jules Barbey d'Aurevilly published a book that was to have a profound effect on his contemporaries, among them Gautier and Baudelaire, and on the later "decadent" generation that included Huysmans. *Du Dandyisme et de Georges Brummell* was a celebratory account and shrewd interpretation of the notorious English Regency figure Beau Brummell, who had settled in France and died there in miserable circumstances in 1840.

Brummell is popularly thought of now as having been merely a clotheshorse; the term "dandy," which he inspired, suggests flamboyance and a fussy concern in matters of male attire, a peacock stance. In actuality, as Ellen Moers tells us in her fine study of the dandy, his style of dress was "so restrained and so natural as to be a triumph of mind over body." It was Brummell's cold fastidiousness and somber elegance that recommended him to Barbey, who saw in him a being who "does not work" but simply exists and is therefore both "a lesson in elegance to the vulgar mind" and a brilliant reproof to the age's thick, indiscriminate materialism. "Barbey points out," Moers says, "that the dandy's distinction, almost his responsibility, is his abhorrence of uniformity, mediocrity and vulgarity." He is a hierophant, a priest of new aristocratic rites, "*un homme*" as Barbey writes, "*qui porte en lui quelque chose du supérieur au monde visible.*"

Charles Péguy, the French Catholic writer who was killed in the first days of World War I, once described what he called the "bourgeois mind" as that which invariably "prefers the visible to the invisible." The "something superior" to the palpable world that Barbey saw Brummell as embodying derived its quasi-mystical power from an unheard-of dedication to his own perfection. It was as if he alone were entitled to determine its constituents and thereby express a scorn for the bourgeoisie's idolatry of objects, its demand for proofs of usefulness, and its ignorance of the true principles of taste.

A scandal to moralists, beyond his subtle and austere appearance (black, gray, and white were his only "colors") Brummell—and the ideal dandy—reserved himself for himself. Indifferent to the crowd, free of any trace of worldly ambition, irresponsible in practical matters, an enemy of utensils, he was, as Moers writes, "ideally free of all human commitments that conflict" with the pure exercise of taste: "passions, moralities, ambitions, politics or occupations." And Barbey saw in this a variation on the role of the artist: "*Il plaisait avec sa personne, comme d'autres plaisaient avec leurs oeuvres.*"

It was the young Baudelaire who seized most quickly and adroitly on the Brummell of Barbey's portrait, converting it to his own uses. Chief among them was precisely the attempt to eliminate the space between the artist's works and the dandy's stance. For Baudelaire, as Michel Butor has written, "dandyism [was] actually only the prefiguration of the poetic state." He took to wearing black, Brummell's badge of austere taste and also, Baudelaire said, the appropriate hue for an age in mourning, in which "we celebrate all that is being buried." His attempt was to take the dandy's freedom from material commitments and passionate entanglements and combine that with the aesthetic impulse to create forms that would exist outside the self. The entire effort was sustained by and enveloped in a mood of unyielding opposition to what he considered vulgarity, the too easily known, the obtusely healthy, the crassly secular and optimistic.

With Baudelaire truly begins what has been called—and in some quarters aggressively proclaimed itself to be—the Decadence in France. Ironies bristle around this origin. He himself thought the word "vague" and too convenient, a cant term to be brandished by "ignorant pedagogues." Yet most of the phenomena it was and is supposed to describe can be traced to him: that is, he is found as the early object of their attribution. That side of "decadence" that is thought to traffic in the grotesque or the sexually bizarre or the freakish, in sensations of exquisite and sterile refinement, in languorous debauchery and cultivated eroticism ("It was Baudelaire," Paul Éluard wrote, "who first noticed the disturbing sensuality in the contrast between the white thighs of cancan dancers and their black stockings")—all this is, or is supposed to be, Baudelaire's province, his spiritual caliphate. He is the source, for those who want to think so, of the imagination gone awry, become sick, and losing its moral base; he is the organizer, it is said, of the modern imagination as cicerone to the perverse.

This is a superficial indictment, an obtuse one in fact. It takes no account of Baudelaire's kind of spirituality, his taking, to begin with, Chateaubriand's aesthetically oriented Catholicism to a far deeper level. For Baudelaire Catholicism was essentially a structure to contain a sense of sin, of moral anxiety and incompleteness; these were conditions of experience which he knew to be largely absent from his age of secular complacency and which he therefore set himself to reintroduce. Standing outside the formal Church, intent, it often seems, on desecration in the interest of sounding an alarm ("His business," T. S. Eliot wrote, "was not to practise Christianity, but—what was much more important for his time—to assert its necessity"), he became for his contemporaries, and even more decisively for the following generation, the man who had raised the most fundamental question of all: what are we to do with our souls in an age that does not recognize their existence?

A narcissist no doubt—a man whose basic attitude, Jean-Paul Sartre says in his strange, mean-spirited book on Baudelaire, was that of someone "bending over himself"—he nevertheless attempted to deal with the problem of the soul in the face of its seeming to have been wiped out by Progress. And he did this by opposing to "ready-made good" an anatomy not so much of evil as of the conditions of the psyche and spirit from which both good and evil arise, often at the same time. He wrote poems which Sartre says are "like substitutes for the creation of the Good which he had renounced." Baudelaire might have replied to this that they were substitutes for Creation itself, like all poetry and art, and that the Good, in so far as it had been renounced—redefined, even— had to yield its fixed, unexamined place in order for the art to be possible.

Sartre might have been expected to find in Baudelaire an exemplary instance of a refusal of engagement, commitment, and "responsibility," an indictment that has followed the so-called decadent through many generations. And indeed he accuses him of bad faith, of a lack of truthfulness in his life, to which Baudelaire might have answered that the important truths of his existence were the materials of his poetry. In any case, his poetry is not to be judged by his moral state. As Proust remarked about him, "there is no fundamental reason why a man should not have a complete comprehension of suffering and still be quite definitely not 'good.'"

Baudelaire once described himself in a wonderful image as "a bell with a crack." Is it too clever to think of the bell as his poetic voice and the crack as his sinful humanity? At any event, he gave to poetry, and so to life, a deepening and renewal. And he did it through what Erich Auerbach calls his "unswerving despair" and "unswerving honesty." Eliot said of him that "what he knew he found out for himself," and this in a time of an especially potent reign of received wisdom and blindly accepted convictions. Is there a better definition of what we call a "culture hero"?

This defense of Baudelaire is not a digression. It is necessary in order to establish a certain measure of innocence for him, in the light of the subsequent guilty taint his reputation takes on from its close embrace with "decadence," that word whose ambiguity and imprecision he understood better than anyone. Linked with it, his poetry and life are forced to point backward, in moral realms, at least, and there is a sense in which this is just. This presenter of the "essential modern man," as Verlaine described him, was indeed searching behind himself for what had been lost. He was, in Georges Poulet's superb phrase, "the poet of the irretrievable," and this impulse toward what cannot be regained, but what must be sought for the survival of the spirit, needs a word other than "decadence" to describe the role it plays in past consciousness and in our own.

Gautier, in his preface to the edition of *Les Fleurs du mal* published in 1868, the year after Baudelaire's death (a preface that was to accompany the only popular edition of the poems for the next fifty years), was the first to call him decadent. As I have said, it had not been a term that had been used to characterize persons, and in fact, in applying it to the poet, Gautier was actually invoking the work, as when we speak, for example, of Shakespeare's qualities and mean the plays' rather than the man's. But the term would quickly slip away from its technical or literary use and come to spread its moral connotation over the man.

Gautier's famous description of the poems is worth quoting at some length. In one especially decisive passage he speaks of "the morbidly rich tints of decomposition, the tones of mother-of-pearl which freeze stagnant waters, the roses of consumption, the pallor of chlorosis, the hateful bilious yellows, the leaden grey of pestilential fogs, the poisoned and metallic greens smelling of sulphide of arsenic . . . the bitumens blacked and browned in the depths of hell, and all that gamut of intensified colors, correspondent to autumn, and the setting of the sun, to overripe fruit, and the last hours of civilization."

This bravura prose set the tone for a great deal of subsequent misreading of Baudelaire, and helped put the Decadent Movement, which largely thought of Baudelaire the way Gautier taught it to—he was his spokesman and self-appointed interpreter, his "publicity agent," someone has said —on a strange, almost accidental course. In its own hyperbole the passage is at least as revealing of Gautier as of his ostensible subject.

Ten years older than Baudelaire, Gautier had been the young leader of a generation for which romanticism was turning into something more complex. Indeed, it was Baudelaire, much influenced by the older man's work, who, more than anyone else, incarnated and spurred on the change. Gautier's *Mademoiselle de Maupin* had deeply affected its generation (its influence would go on to Swinburne and Wilde in England, a text for "decadence" there) by its theme of seductive, impossible aspiration—its heroine wants to be a man, for example—and its positing of a rarefied, uncompromising beauty, an antidote to the vulgar age. He had been the creator, Maxime du Camp said, of a "sort of imaginary nature."

But Gautier had surprisingly little sensitivity to or sympathy for Baudelaire's real concerns. An enormously cultivated man, an artist with as highly developed and unaccommodating an aesthetic sense as anybody in the century until Mallarmé, his was a mind to which the perpetual moral crisis in which Baudelaire lived, the unending anguish and doubt, were almost entirely foreign. For Baudelaire, "decadence" or what might be taken for it, was primarily a matter of metaphysical inquiry and leaning; for Gautier it was a style, a coloration, and an attitude.

He was a pagan, it might be said, a conjuror of celebratory rites in the sunlight, and from his influence the Decadent Movement took several of its cues: its nostalgia for the flamboyant past, for the *terribilità* of dying civilizations, whose despair it turned into gorgeous nightmares, and also its neoromantic hunger for the impossible experience. Along with this it also took from Baudelaire a direction toward the blasphemous and execratory, toward sinfulness as perilous wisdom.

If Baudelaire, then, came to represent that side of Decadence which was of a moral or spiritual order, the examination and cultivation of the forbidden, the tainted, in a realm of injured or arrested souls and of voluptuous blasphemy, Gautier was the chief progenitor of what we might call its secular side, its more "physical" and also more romantic one. His influence was felt in the growing nostalgia for what were considered to have been more robust and dramatic ages, including their violent fates, in a penchant for the colorful and outlandish (Gautier wore crimson and orange clothing, flowing ties; Baudelaire remained in black), in bohemianism and artistic snobbery.

It would be foolish to say that the intellectual and cultural process by which Decadence became an identifiable literary and artistic current in France owed all its spirit and strategies directly to these two figures. Such developments are, naturally, enormously complex—Mario Praz's *Romantic Agony* offers literally hundreds of sources for the movement. There may have been any number of Decadent poets and novelists, to say nothing of graphic artists, who had scarcely read a word of either writer. But the two were prime contributors to the cultural atmosphere, and even when as conscious forces they disappeared from time to time behind the crowd of newcomers—poseurs, incompetents, or authentic voices as these variously might have been—they held their places as tutors and releasers of imaginative force.

Perhaps the key notion in Gautier's encomium to *Les Fleurs du mal* was that of "overripeness." It was this quality he found so arresting in ancient societies during their decline, and it recommended itself to him because it stood in antithesis to the chief qualities of his own age, as he saw them. His time was energetic, to be sure, but the energy went into production, not creation; it was a cold, measured, wholly unlyrical and monochromatic age that gave the imagination no purchase on the fabulous, the vivid, and no space in which to construct dreams. Its health was therefore a type of sickness to the creative person, a sterility for which the cure was thought to be corruption and excess. (A later writer, Italo Svevo, would also employ the idea of the superiority of sickness in a vulgarly healthy world, but for him it was a literary strategy, not a program, and he used it unromantically, with an irony and sly humor such as Gautier seems entirely to have lacked.)

In *La Nuit de Cléopatre*, Gautier gave expression to a sentiment that would gain in force as the century went on, as one mode of escape from and protest against the age of progress, the time of philistinism, rationality, and tight measure. "Our world is very small beside the ancient world," he wrote, "our feasts are paltry affairs compared with the terrifying banquets of Roman patricians and Asiatic princes. With our petty habits, we find it hard to conceive of those enormous existences which made reality of all the strangest, boldest, most monstrously impossible inventions of our imaginations."

This fascination with what was thought to be the greater imaginative size of the ancient world, its sensual vigor and capacity for extreme pleasures, fed from many sources and displayed itself in both subtly refined and extraordinarily coarse ways. The mind went back once again to the Greco-Roman world, but not this time for its classical virtues. What was admired in that largely dreamed-up human universe was its excesses, its "violent splendors," its life closer to the bone which was at the same time far more elaborate and brilliantly artificial than the present. The prototypes were Caligula, Nero, Heliogabalus, Messalina.

At the Salon of 1847 a painting by Thomas Couture caused a great sensation. It portrayed a fanciful scene of Roman debauchery, the patricians at their revels, with busts of ancestors looking on in stern disapproval. The picture, which was called *The Romans of the Decadence,* bore a warning subtitle from Juvenal—"Luxury has fallen upon us, more terrible than the sword, and the conquered East has revenged herself with the gift of her vices." But this gesture was happily ignored and the tone was established for several generations of exotic neoclassical kitsch. Beyond that, the word "decadence" achieved a new and flamboyant currency.

Alexandria of the third and fourth centuries and, especially, Byzantium, with its hedonism and gorgeous heavy styles of architecture and ornament, in time replaced Rome at the center of this neoromantic longing. This nostalgia was an appetite for what was felt to be lacking in the present, a strange desire for depravity and corruption seen as liberating; it was a desire for a stasis of the senses and the soul in a grandeur of repletion. At its most legitimate, in the imaginations of those for whom the present was mechanically and reductively brutal, the cult of the violent, fateful past provided a ground for a renewed sense of passionate life, or at least a tactic toward its recovery. Even so, it was mixed with nonsense.

Flaubert was one of those caught between authentic feeling and foolish dreams. To his fervor for that Mediterranean history which must have seemed almost a prehistory, a time before the rationalization of life, he added a hunger for the East, the place of timelessness and, one could fancy, extended miracles of the senses. "The East," he rhapsodized, "its vast deserts . . . its palaces trodden by camels . . . mares bounding towards the sun-flushed horizons . . . blue waves, clear sky and silvery sand . . . the smell of warm oceans . . . and then, near me, in a tent shaded by a broad-leaved aloe, some brown-skinned woman with burning eyes who would hold me in her arms and whisper the language of the houris." Flaubert could not have written this kind of thing without Gautier's example. But the infection was by that time widespread.

To trace the career of an abstract and judgmental word such as "decadence" is to feel the urge to seize on every hard, specific date that turns up, before one is swept away again into the seas of the unrecorded. All historical study is of course dependent on documents, especially those we can date, but intellectual history is almost wholly so. We cannot know, for example, that an idea has existed until we see it expressed. The word "sexuality," to take a not so remote example, seems to have been first used in the 1840s by Kierkegaard, who meant by it an indication that something had changed in consciousness about sex; it had been removed to the condition of a subject for study and concern. He was the first, as far as we know, to identify this shift, but was he the first to have noticed it?

Moreover, the changing uses of words are changes in ideas. A word such as "heretic" passes from the religious sphere to that of politics, say, or one like "politics" from government to intrigue in business or the academy. In cases of this kind the possibility of discovering the first of the new usages is remote, to say the least. What is more difficult still is to determine the relationship between the new use and the old, when the differences are acute and the established use has retained its potency. To chart movements in language accurately is a hopeless ideal; everything is speculation, approximation, likelihood, and inference, and "evidence" is simply what has emerged from all that remains hidden. The archaeology of language is a thin science.

The evidence, then, is that "decadence" became a proper noun with increasing currency sometime between about 1870 and 1880 and that shortly afterward it began to be applied as an adjective to details of personal behavior such as it had seldom been used to describe before. As a capitalized word it became a label only after the fact. Frenchmen of the period, the nonprofessionally intellectual or artistic at any rate, were not profoundly conscious of living in the "French Decadance," however often the term was wielded by thinkers in love with categories. Are we aware, in any way that really affects us, of living in a "post-Freudian" age or, in regard to artistic questions, in a "post-modernist" one? These are classifications for textbooks and invariably miss the truth they are after.

"Decadence" was part of the atmosphere. At the same time as the word was changing into something categorical and gaining new significances and references, it went on asserting the old, so that for a strange length of confused time it was simultaneously a term of disapprobation and a rallying cry.

There are historians who argue that the word's new status as a pejorative, especially in political and social matters, was due to the calamitous events with which the decade began in France: the defeat at the hands of Prussia and the agony of the Paris Commune. The word had for a long time been in the political air, but now its use greatly increased and it took on a new and far more apocalyptic intensity. "The Republic or Decadence!" "Religion or Decadence!" "Equality or Decadence!" Slogans like these were actually brandished by extremists in the political struggles of the time. It was as though the mystery of communal suffering could be apprehended and a hope of healing be maintained only through a formulation in which the comparative solidity and clarity of a familiar institution or a political bias was opposed to the darkness and unfathomable loss of footing that was thought to be summarized in the latter word.

At the same time "decadence" was becoming more and more both a catchword and a serious, almost hieratic designation in art and literature. As I have said, Gautier had called Baudelaire decadent, and the latter had emerged after his death as the powerful, unrivaled tutor of a new generation's sensibilities. As is so often the case in matters of evaluative language, the word was immediately seized on within the artistic and intellectual world from different perspectives and with subtly or grossly differing intentions. From this split arose the subsequent ambiguity of the term, the confusion over its meaning even on the part of those who regarded it as a signal of praise.

The founding in 1886 by Anatole Baju of a literary and cultural journal called *Le Décadent* was one of those familiar programmatic acts in the intellectual realm in which sincerity and egoism are inextricably mixed. Something has been noticed in the air, a current or a tendency, and now it is announced, made explicit and, inevitably, turned into a fashion. Many of the young poets and aesthetes who made up the magazine's circle doubtless had a passionate belief in the virtue of their cause—which was to proclaim and celebrate what they considered to be a new sensibility, tuned to extravagance, to the grotesque but also to the refined, to the exquisite and unworldly, and facing away from the bourgeois age. But there must have been at least as many who simply seized the opportunity to draw attention to themselves.

That the journal was short-lived, as such enterprises generally are, was due in part to its "insincerity," its use of cultural engagement for self-aggrandizement or arid celebrity. Deeper than that, its importance was largely symptomatic, as we can now see, because the energies and values it sought to represent and advance—or those it sought to oppose—were far greater and more complex than its formulary approach could hope to contain. Its pages were filled with proclamations, calls to order, and that peculiar fusion of aggressive certainty and plaintive wishfulness which characterizes so many *soi-disant* movements in thought and the arts. "Man is growing more refined, more feminine, more divine," one of *Le Décadent*'s writers declared. Behind the assertion lay a disgust with the brutal, materialistic, "masculine" age, and a kernel of objective truth: some artists, not all of them men, were moving toward what they hoped would be an alternative epoch of the senses.

For Baju, an otherwise undistinguished littérateur, the time was fully ripe. Between 1880 and 1883 Paul Bourget had written a series of influential *Essais de psychologie contemporaine* in which, among other things, he had drawn attention to writers like Baudelaire, Gautier, and the Goncourt brothers, praising them for having created a style adapted to what he considered a decaying society. Bourget was a conservative who deplored the growing fragmentation of contemporary life and the new stress on individual consciousness, yet he defended Decadence as a position, calling it, as Konrad Swart has written, "intellectually and esthetically, if not ethically and socially superior" to the prevailing ethos. The essays did much to make Decadence respectable as a literary attitude and program.

In 1883 the publication in *Le Décadent* of Paul Verlaine's poem "Longueur" was greeted enthusiastically by a number of like-minded poets; it was also hailed as a masterpiece by the critic Félicien Chapsaur, who then proceeded to group Verlaine and his admirers and acolytes into a school of Decadence. Verlaine quickly slipped away, at least to the extent that he repudiated the appellation, although he continued to reign, in his café-monarch fashion, over those younger poets and writers who aggressively accepted it. But the impulse had now become a more or less official movement.

From then on, everything unfolded with the untidiness and confusion that marks all cultural progression and makes intellectual history so difficult to master and to write: advances and retreats, appearances and disappearances, avowals and repudiations, temporary marriages of opposites and sunderings of old connections and, most disconcerting of all, terminologies shifting almost from moment to moment, words emptying out and filling up again, pressed from behind by changed intentions, new strategies, hopefulness, invented needs.

In 1885, before the term had even taken full hold, some of the younger Decadents began to call themselves Symbolists, getting their cue, of course, from Mallarmé. As Baudelaire and Gautier had stood between Romanticism and Decadence, Mallarmé stood between Decadence and all the movements that succeeded it. We use the word "movements," but this is only a convenient term for cultural activities that share certain characteristics. There never was a time, as intellectual historians crave and, succumbing, sometimes invent, when Decadence showed itself in clean lines, set off from the rest of art and thought. And there never was a time when Decadence was definitive, since nobody agreed on what the definitions were. What existed were figures, works, unloosed visions.

In his critique of the Salon of 1889, Joris-Karl Huysmans paid special, heated attention to the paintings of Gustave Moreau, employing a descriptive vocabulary at least as violent and apocalyptic as the aesthetic visions he was dealing with. This vocabulary would appear at first glance to have been one of negation and distaste; yet its estimates and images were subtly admiring, in that mode of a reversal of the normal and conventionally healthy which Decadence had put forward.

"Spiritual onanism," Huysmans wrote of Moreau, "a soul exhausted by secret thoughts . . . insidious appeals to sacrilege and debauchery . . . goddesses riding hippographs and streaking with their lapis-lazuli wings the death-agony of the clouds . . . The crushed globes of bleeding suns and hemorrhages of stars flowing in crimson cataracts . . . Contrary to Taine's dictum environment stimulates revolt; exceptional individuals retrace their steps down the centuries, and, out of disgust for the promiscuities they have to suffer, hurl themselves into the abyss of bygone ages, into the tumultuous spaces of dreams and nightmares."

Huysmans and Moreau. In these two figures the last generation of the century, the one that has carried the designation "decadent" ever since, seemed to find the exact intersection of all the lines of feeling and spiritual rumor that had been extending through the air for so long. Moreau, the older man, was, like Huysmans, a visionary-moralist, though in both cases the latter quality has been difficult to see behind the mantic surfaces. For all his dislike of certain aspects of Baudelaire's practice, Moreau might have been chosen to meet the poet's objection to the painting of his time: "From day to day art diminishes its self-respect, prostrates itself before exterior reality, and the artist becomes more and more inclined to paint not what he dreams but what he sees." In Huysmans, Moreau found reflected in a sympathetic eye his own hatred for the modern age and his thirst for archaic "unreality."

In turn Des Esseintes, the protagonist of Huysmans' novel *À Rebours,* speaks of Moreau as the creator of "hieratic and sinister allegories made more to the point by the uneasy perceptions of a nervous system altogether modern in its morbid sensitiveness . . . his work was always painful, haunted by the symbols of superhuman loves and superhuman vices, divine abominations committed without enthusiasm and without hope."

Whether or not Huysmans' diagnosis was wholly correct—he seems to have missed the veiled didacticism of the paintings, their warning note—he was right in his notion of a "modern" neurosis that was observable in Moreau. This idea of an unprecedented present moment of spiritual unrest and psychic ambiguity was deeply characteristic of that elaborately self-conscious age. Verlaine had identified Baudelaire as the first portraitist of a new, wholly problematic type of man, and his generation now found Huysmans and Moreau to be sources of themes and images of those strange, unstable new combinations of personality and instinct which were what was chiefly meant by neurosis and in some ways still are. Nothing was more prominent in this regard than the figure of the *femme fatale,* Salome and her type, and that of the androgyne. Both were major elements of Moreau's iconography, and of the larger atmosphere of Decadent imagination.

Des Esseintes saw in Moreau's Salome the "weird and superhuman figure he had dreamed of . . . [in] the spectacle of her quivering breasts, heaving belly and tossing thighs . . . she was now revealed . . . as the symbolic incarnation of old-world Vice, the goddess of immortal hysteria, the Curse of Beauty supreme above all other beauties by the cataleptic spasm that stirs her flesh and steels her muscles—a monstrous Beast of the Apocalypse, indifferent, irresponsible, insensible, poisoning, like Helen of Troy of the old fables, all who come near her, all who see her, all who touch her."

If the diction of this and much of Huysmans' other, earlier writing may have been learned chiefly from Gautier, it was Baudelaire who was Huysmans' true spiritual mentor, the writer who had made his sensibility possible. That both men should have addressed their complex intellects to an art different from their own (they are two of the best critics of painting of the century) is only the most superficial of the connections between them.

As Ellen Moers has written, Huysmans was quick to acknowledge that Baudelaire was his "predecessor in *la psychologie morbide*." He saw in the earlier writer a model for and instigation to his own "leap toward the fantastic and toward the dream." And when he wrote that "it was through a glimpse of the supernatural of evil that I first obtained insight into the supernatural of good" he identified himself with Baudelaire in a spiritual engagement that the latter, so wary of the categorical and of being thought sententious, could not have professed for himself. "Behind [Huysmans'] finest pages," Barbey d'Aurevilly wrote, "one can feel [Baudelaire's] presence, like a glowing fire."

Huysmans made the connection between Moreau (as well as with Symbolism in its most general aspects) and Baudelaire when he gave Des Esseintes the following reflection: "There breathed from his pictures, so despairing and so erudite, a sorcery that moved you to the bottom of the soul, like that of certain of Baudelaire's poems, and you were left amazed, pensive, disconcerted by this art." His homage to Baudelaire is even more pointedly expressed in the triptych containing three poems from *Les Fleurs du mal* which is a centerpiece of Des Esseintes' living room. But the novel bears the mark of Baudelaire throughout, from its title to its affinities with Poe's "Fall of the House of Usher," which had been made available to Huysmans' generation through Baudelaire's translation and which, along with the rest of Poe's translated work, he saw largely through Baudelaire's eyes.

Everything seemed to converge and dispose itself in Huysmans' fiction and criticism as integral parts of a blasphemous new vision, an extension of that counter-universe, which had been taking shape for years, opposed both to scientific rationalism and the entire humanistic tradition in literature and the other arts. Catholic belief degenerating (or being recklessly brought over) into the cult of Satanism; neurasthenia and sexual perversity; boredom combined with exquisite refinement; nostalgia for the corrupt; fascination with the splendors and despairs of ancient cultures; hatred of the "natural" as the enemy of human invention and transcendence; "progress" as an anathema; taste as a means of survival: it all went to compose a paradigm of "decadence" and has come down to us in that large outline.

But what if this work represented, not the expression of a fixed moral and psychological state, a category of behavior and attitude such as we have been accustomed to define as decadence, but something essentially literary, devised, in a certain sense willed, and in another related and peculiarly telling sense "unreal"? There is a remark of Aubrey Beardsley which is a clue to Huysmans' relation to both Decadence and the decadent. When asked about his strange, "unhealthy" visions, Beardsley replied that "I never allow myself to see them except on paper." The drawing paper bore the reality; literature, like St. Paul's faith, is the evidence of things unseen.

Paul Valéry, who as a young man passionately admired Huysmans' books, wrote about him from a distance and summoned up the man indistinguishably from the work. "There hung about him," he said, "an emanation of strange learning, seasoned with a medley of all the combined superstitions of the writers of his time and group, those of government employees, of the petite bourgeoisie, and of ladies far gone in piety, hovering between heresy and dementia . . . He had a nose for every brand of dirt, evil and shame in all the affairs of this world . . . His strange, palpitating nostrils smelled out everything that was nauseating . . . and he may have been right."

This last speculation is exceedingly odd and ambiguous. Does Valéry mean that Huysmans may have been justified in having appointed himself a hound for the times, having discovered in himself a peculiarly developed tracker's sense? Or does the rightness consist in what he found, what was there to be found and is always there? The matter is a crucial one, a pivot on which much of our understanding of "decadence" may turn. For the relation of decadence, so called, to evil or perversity, its status as an *attraction,* a choice of behavior and self-definition against the prevailing moral (or psychic) grain, is what has always been in question ever since the word began to be used in other than political or sociological contexts.

To begin with, from the testimony of those who knew him, Huysmans, a minor government employee for most of his life, was in actuality a mild, affable, almost diffident man. To say this is in the first place to try to set him free from the vulgar realm in which personality is supposed to determine imagination and the reverse. For the odor of vice which Valéry rightly detected came neither from his person nor from his habits, not even from his speech. Rather, it seems almost blindingly obvious to say, it came from his work. He didn't pursue evil and shameful acts—and everything depends on the fact that he didn't—as either an acolyte or a talented gossip. What truly serious writer has ever done that? Instead, immersed like Baudelaire in the mysteries of moral possibility, conscious to an agonizing degree of the relations between evil and blind, unexamined good, he set himself to identify the nauseating and then build an imaginary, a *literary* barrier around it and against it.

A novel like *À Rebours,* the "bible of the Decadence," as it was so widely proclaimed, is a structure of the most precise artifice and not a blueprint for a "real" life; within its pages, life is carried on at its most artificial, which is to say its most "invented" and refractory to imposed moral and social obligations. "Artifice was considered by Des Esseintes," Huysmans writes on behalf of his creation, "to be the distinctive mark of human genius."

The book *Against Nature,* in the free but actually more pointed English translation, is against it in a double sense. The more obvious one is that which is expressed in Huysmans' sentiment, shared with so many of his contemporaries, that "the beauty of a landscape resides in its melancholy." The more profound is that which is opposed to Nature in its condition as an *idea,* a human system or category, wherein the natural becomes the inevitable disposition of things, the morally sanctified, the given and unchallengeable conditions of life. "Nature," in the bourgeois dimension, is all that it would be unthinkable to challenge. The corollary is that art, as well as radical religion, both being modes of non-acquiescence in the given, are the enemies seeking to overthrow all traditional acceptances.

The point is that what Valéry called the nauseating in human affairs—crime, perversion, the corrupt and tainted— were not ends in themselves for Huysmans, not even as objects of contemplation (as sexual violence was not for Sade), but emblems or reminders of a deeper nausea, that which is produced in certain persons by an awareness of human self-division. The nauseating, the morally inverse, appears in this light as the betrayal of ideality, of unitary being and wholeness in the self, an ascription which in a theological perspective becomes that of original sin. But it follows from this that such nausea may afford a sense of the self such as the merely pious and conventionally moral can never know, and that it may testify, the way darkness does to light, to the possibility, even the imminence, of its opposite.

It would seem to have been that the shameful and repellent, as well as the blasphemous—which is what is nauseating to the believer—were, for Huysmans, unexpected evidence of life; they were signs of active besieged existence beneath the formulas of civilization, most crucially beneath the falsely authoritative, smug notion of progress. When a character in *Là Bas* asserts that "I learned long ago that there are no people interesting to know except saints, scoundrels and crackpots," the moral world is framed and redefined by its extremes, with the bland "lifeless" middle conjured away.

It is not that Huysmans was unafflicted, any more than were

Des Esseintes and his other surrogates or, more to the point, his own invented personae. They are victims of the age as much as they are its critics or defiers. But there is a sense in which the true critic or prophet has to carry in himself the infection of the time, holding it in solution, so to speak, perhaps even being its first or chief carrier in this way. It was Baudelaire's spiritual malady, his incapacity for faith together with his acute recognition of its necessity, that helped make him the kind of prophetic writer he was. And it was Huysmans' extraordinary receptivity to the spiritual crisis of his own time that made him its foremost chronicler, its first forthright though half-unwilling celebrant.

Most of Huysmans' contemporaries saw him as incarnating the quintessential qualities of the Decadent Period, and many saw his work as the last powerful manifestation of a process of inexorable literary decline. As it turned out, and so often turns out in the case of so-called literary decadence, his books were actually the first statements of a wholly new literary movement. Jules Lemaître spoke of him as a "very determined, very conscious and refined" artist, the "*détraqué* representative of the extreme tendencies of a literature nearing its end." And Barbey d'Aurevilly said that for a Huysmans to have been produced "it was necessary that we should have become what in fact we are—a race which has reached its final hour." Yet a much more shrewd and accurate assessment was offered by Rémy de Gourmont, who without the perfervid rhetoric so characteristic of the time, and of French cultural pronouncements at any time, spoke of *A Rebours* as "a book which has stated in advance, and for a long time to come, our loves and our hates."

Freer than most of his contemporaries of an intellectual or

temperamental stake in the existence of decadence as a category of behavior or as a program, aware of the word's singular status as a descriptive without determinable substance, de Gourmont was able to see Huysmans as neither decadent nor enervated but prophetic. It may be overstating the case for Huysmans to say, as Cyril Connolly did, that he and Mallarmé created the modern sensibility between them, but to place him at the beginning of a line is far more just than to fix him at the end of one.

One more event needs to be noted. It isn't a proof that Huysmans was not decadent, in the pejorative sense of the word, that he reconverted to Catholicism, that his late works celebrated a movement toward a center, toward an orthodoxy, brilliantly figured and intellectually demanding as orthodoxy only rarely is. But it is a sign of something more subtle and complex than our categories can hope to encompass. He once described his earlier writing as "naturalistic spirituality." In this light his "decadence" can be seen as one fertile side or phase of a psychic, moral, and intellectual destiny that unfolded through the dialectic such internal careers always possess. The movement is neither forward nor backward but around a center.

And yet, more than any other figure of the French Decadence, Huysmans continues to give off an emanation of perversity and of febrile, arcane sensuality. These were the qualities that recommended him to the more shallow among his admirers in France, and they were the ones that carried his reputation, or notoriety, across the Channel. In the late eighties Huysmans, with Baudelaire, became a chief instigator of a brief cultural climate in England, called at the beginning the Aesthetic Movement but as time went on more and more referred to as the Decadence, too. Thinner than its French counterpart, less passionate and ideological, it was yet marked by many of the same aspirations and by much the same confusion and cloudiness surrounding its governing idea and word.

4

"IN HOURS LIKE THESE A PAGE OF HUYSMANS is as a dose of opium, a glass of some exquisite and powerful liqueur," George Moore wrote in his journal at the end of the 1880s. Moore, a busy cultural acolyte, poet, novelist, and Francophile, reflected in his *Confessions of a Young Man* (1888) on another central influence upon his and other British imaginations of the period:

The study of Baudelaire aggravated the course of the disease. No longer is it the grand barbaric face of Gautier; now it is the clean-shaven face of the mock priest, the slow, cold eyes and the sharp cunning sneer of the cynical libertine who will be tempted that he may better know the worthlessness of temptation. "Les Fleurs du Mal!" Beautiful flowers in sublime decay . . . the children of the nineteenth century go to you, O Baudelaire, and having tasted of your deadly delights all hope of repentance is vain.

Moore's testimony is of course excessive and even ludicrous and displays a conventional misreading of Baudelaire. Still, its themes of spiritual malaise, fatal enchantment, and seduction by the idea of corruption were precisely those that attracted a type of inexperienced Anglo-Saxon mind to the French. His words show us what it was like for an impressionable young writer, raised in the Victorian atmosphere of repressed passion, moral hypocrisy, and fear of "dangerous" art, to come upon Baudelaire and the whole startling line of *poètes maudits*.

There had been a much more admirable and clear-headed—

but far less influential—strain of appreciation of Baudelaire in England. In 1875 George Saintsbury had offered an estimate of the French poet that went to the heart of the differences between the practice of literature in England and in France:

It is not merely admiration of Baudelaire which is to be persuaded to English readers, but also imitation of him which is with at least equal earnestness to be urged upon English writers. We have had in England authors in every kind not to be surpassed in genius, but we have always lacked more or less the class of *écrivains artistes*—writers who have recognized that writing is an art, and who have applied themselves with the patient energy of sculptors, painters and musicians to the discovery of its secrets.

Such sober advice was not likely to overcome the more emotional and melodramatic side of Baudelaire's effect on English sensibility, nor that of his successors such as Huysmans and Verlaine. In 1862 Swinburne published the first English translations of poems from *Les Fleurs du mal*. From then on, "advanced" British consciousness, especially the literary side of it, was powerfully affected—though seldom with full comprehension of what it was undergoing—by the movement into hitherto suppressed regions of the psyche and imagination, the aggressive stance against bourgeois proprieties and dogmas and the turning of "negative" subjects into materials for art that had been so largely initiated in France and that had culminated in her so-called Decadence.

Still, the "Yellow Nineties," which make up the English counterpart of the *fin de siècle* in France, were given the provocative name through a chance circumstance: the exotic French novels that had begun to have a vogue in London during the previous decade happened to have been bound mostly in that color. In Oscar Wilde's novel, Dorian Gray's education in vice is helped along by a "poisonous book" in a yellow cover which Wilde later acknowledged had been inspired by Huysmans' *À Rebours,* as indeed had the whole narrative. And so when a year or two later the entrepreneurs of the new (and, as it turned out, short-lived) monthly that has come down to us as the decade's representative journal were casting about for a name, *The Yellow Book* recommended itself with a certain flair. The decade then took its name from that.

That the magazine proved to be far less dangerous and subversive of established culture and morals than its name's provenance might suggest (it was in fact surprisingly tame, even bland, much more so than its lesser known rival and successor, the *Savoy*) is less interesting than the fact that it should have been given the name in the first place. What lay behind it was that to its literary practitioners—if the word doesn't suggest an assiduousness and professional zeal that were only seldom the case—and its decriers alike, the so-called English Decadence, which reached its full and brief expression in the late eighties and early nineties, owed, as Moore testified, much of its inspiration, a good many of its specific themes, and even a leading part of its vocabulary— "ennui," "spleen," "languor"—to French models and precepts.

What such indebtedness meant and usually means is rather different from the word's ordinary implications. Nobody, of any seriousness at least, would have confessed to literally borrowing from the French, turning out English transcriptions of French poetry or fiction, say, or choosing his clothes or domestic decor in strict obedience to handbooks published in Paris. Cultural influence of this kind generally appears to those who succumb to it, however imitative they may become in practice, as a remarkable and inspiriting coincidence of one's own desires and intuitions with artistic or intellectual achievements reached elsewhere: *it can be this way* and ought to be, is the lesson of the encounter. The effect of the experience can be sober, a reasoned propulsion of the mind and spirit, or it can be romantic, even apocalyptic, as it was for George Moore.

Whichever it was in particular cases, the effect of the French exemplars upon English minds is familiar enough as cultural history. What is not so well known is the influence the English had earlier exerted on the French and continued to exert in certain areas, especially painting and design, until well into the nineties and even beyond. Blake's mysticism and "madness," for example, had perhaps been more appreciated in France than at home, and a poem like Keats's "La Belle Dame sans Merci," with its motif of the fatal woman and its reminder to the French of one aspect of their own earlier imaginative history, lay at the back of much mid-century French obsession along those lines.

Less directly an artistic influence, but still a central element in the atmosphere in which artists and would-be artists composed their stances, was the English phenomenon of the dandy. This had been transported to France by Beau Brummell himself when he took up residence there in 1816, and it had strongly influenced Gautier, Barbey d'Aurevilly, and Baudelaire among many other writers. Finally, the Pre-Raphaelite mood of nostalgia for earlier, more "spiritual" ages, and certain elements of Pre-Raphaelite style, had a measurable effect on the French Decadent and Symbolist painters and on *fin-de-siècle* neo-Romanticism in general.

Still, by the sixties the tide was running heavily in the other direction. Aptly enough, it was Swinburne who was later to carry across the water the "infection," as proper Victorian literary opinion considered it. Along with his promotion of Baudelaire, Swinburne was also among the first in England to adopt Baudelaire's own spiritual ancestors and confrères, Sade and Gautier, whose *Mademoiselle de Maupin,* a book that Oscar Wilde later also admired, Swinburne called "the holy writ of beauty."

Swinburne, a splendid and important poet in many respects, was a highly unstable personality, intellectually a peculiar combination of daring, schoolboyish bravado and subterranean priggishness, emotionally a retarded being, a flirter with moral danger and a cultivator of perversions whose real nature he seems scarcely to have understood and from whose grip he was able to extricate himself only by retreating into a life of almost total sensual deprivation. Nothing would be sillier than to hold him responsible for the more juvenile aspects of the nineties in England, but there is something to be said for his having provided certain models of rhetoric and behavior.

When T. S. Eliot in a well-known essay on Baudelaire said of Swinburne that he "knew nothing about Evil, or Vice, or Sin," one of his meanings was surely that Swinburne's knowledge of them was not comparable to that of his French mentors, the religious or invertedly religious ones at least. Had he known, Eliot went on, "he would not have had so much fun out of it." In this context, "having fun" is rather unfair and certainly misleading; it would be more accurate to say that Swinburne and his disciples and spiritual descendants of the eighties and nineties *played at* evil and sin, experimenting, with the fascinated stare, the tentative movements, the backing and filling, the jibes and japes, and finally the awareness of being in over one's head that characterizes the sexually adolescent in matters of this kind—a particular sort of cultural adolescence, too. And Swinburne was much more aware of his "inauthenticity" than Eliot recognized, as a little poem of his testifies:

> Some singers indulging in curses,
> Though sinful, have splendidly sinned,
> But my would-be maleficent verses
> Are nothing but wind.

Nothing could be more revealing of the contrast between French complexity and English immaturity in this realm of experience than the names that have been formally applied to the more or less contemporaneous cultural climates or intellectual tides in the two countries: the Decadent Movement in France and the Aesthetic one in England. ("Decadent" came to be more and more used in England as the French influence became obvious and conservatives grew alarmed.) Although the reality contained its share of passion and authentic spirit, the very term "Aesthetic Movement" smacks of amateurism and the dilettantish, of something earnest and high-minded, almost hygienic. When Oscar Wilde called Walter Pater a "Presbyterian Verlaine," he was not being entirely unfair.

Still, Pater and the Aesthetic Movement were as revolutionary and original as any artistic consciousness England could produce during the period, and as close to French thought and taste—in so far as it wished to be—as anybody could have expected, in the light of the wide differences of national temperament and experience. Unlike Swinburne, Pater played no direct role in the transmission to England of French art and ideas, but stood rather as a mind less immediately affected by those things than as one exhibiting certain strong natural affinities with some of their aspects. From this Oxford don, with his strange, elegant, frozen sensibility, English writers and artists learned a cultivation of consciousness such as they had never heard preached with such gravity and conviction, a cultivation of sensation, and what Pater called "the fascination of corruption."

In *The Decadent Movement in Literature,* Arthur Symons spoke of Pater's *Studies in the Renaissance* and *Marius the Epicurean* as having "that morbid subtlety of analysis, that morbid curiosity of form that we have found in the world of the French Decadents." And Mario Praz, in *The Romantic Agony,* speaks of the "climate" of Pater's books as containing the very essence of decadence: "His inspiration remained almost motionless throughout his life, as if spellbound by the image of some rich and melancholy adolescence."

The qualities of morbidity and arrested growth which Symons and Praz associated with decadence make up ripe grounds for suspicion, since they hint at criteria of "healthiness" and orderly development such as have been the basis for a great deal of reactionary aesthetic opinion throughout history. But whatever his "decadence" might have consisted of, Pater was undoubtedly a major force in shaping the Aesthetic Movement along lines that brought it closer to its more complex and radical counterpart in France. He would be greatly troubled later by the excesses and follies of the nineties, particularly the scandals created by Wilde's homosexuality, but his influence remained central even then.

There were, of course, other native sources for the development, among them the rediscovery of Blake and Keats as visionary, prophetic ancestors. Swinburne's study of Blake, published in the 1860s, may have been overblown and even perverse (he found strong affinities between Blake and Sade), but his emphasis on the British poet's "holy insurrection," his vision of humanity's control of its spiritual and moral destiny, greatly recommended itself to a generation seeking deliverance from what it thought of as brutal physical power and utilitarian ideals.

The Pre-Raphaelite movement figured largely, too, and after that, most centrally, there were the writings of John Ruskin, who in an age of sober material considerations taught a passionate commitment to beauty, to craftsmanship regarded as noble and self-justifying, and to an idea of the past, especially the medieval age, as having realized its particular nature most fully through the arts.

In the imagination of the generation that included Oscar Wilde, Ruskin's sermons about the high importance of art and its superiority to bourgeois values fused with the stress that Pater (with most of whose ideas Ruskin felt no sympathy) had placed on the need for new experience. An additional element of the intellectual weather was provided by James Whistler, who in his talk and practice came as close as anyone in England ever had to promulgating a doctrine of *l'art pour l'art*.

The "pure" imagination, the imagination uncoerced by the weightiness and apparent sovereignty of fact, had not since the Jacobeans been a major element of English artistic energies. This new enthusiasm for the independence of art from political, social, and, at the extreme edge, moral actuality already filled the air, then, when Oscar Wilde, who was to take some aspects of aestheticism as far as they would go and give "decadence" an English definition and coloration, made his arch, rollicking, Pied Piperish, ill-fated appearance upon the scene.

The main events of Wilde's career and ultimate downfall are too familiar to need recounting here. He began his public life, he told a friend just before he left Oxford, with the ambition of becoming a "poet, a writer, a dramatist. Somehow or other I'll be famous, and if not famous I'll be notorious." As we know, he became both. One of his deft feats was to create from the beginning an image of himself larger and more flamboyant than the reality. Bunthorne in Gilbert and Sullivan's *Patience* sang mockingly of walking "down Piccadilly with a poppy or a lily in your medieval hand," as Wilde was supposed to have done, to which he used to say, "anyone could have done that. The difficult thing to achieve was to make people think that I had done it."

His own "aesthetic" period in dress and manner lasted only a few years, although its celebrity endured: at the height of his fame he wore no extravagant or flamboyant clothing, and the great fur coat that he had bought for his American tour had long been in storage. By the time he achieved full recognition he was able to rule by his wit and the rumor of his wit. From having been an "outrageous" figure in the sense of exclamations accompanied by amused or baffled headshakings—"Oh, that Oscar Wilde, what will he say (or do) next?"—he rose, or descended, to the status of a monster, a source of rage. From having been the archetypal aesthete of his day he became its representative decadent, with the far more disturbing implications of that term.

Although they were to be found in English dictionaries, "decadent" and "decadence" had not been words that many Englishmen, even educated ones, were ever likely to have used, and then only as a more or less formal term to describe large issues of the condition of society or civilization. As the cultural winds came across the Channel, the word began to take on the titillating, vaguely immoral quality some Anglo-Saxons still tend vulgarly to associate with things French. The upholders of Victorian morality, in literature as well as in wider spheres, now began to employ it as a weapon in their arsenal of invective against the disturbing new currents. Swinburne had been attacked for his French influences and tastes, the "unnatural passions," the "blasphemy," and now with Wilde's *Picture of Dorian Gray* (1891) the alarm was fully sounded. "It is a . . . morbid . . . unhealthy . . . tale spawned from the leprous literature of the French decadent," wrote a reviewer in the *Daily Chronicle,* "a poisonous book . . . heavy with the mephitic odour of moral and spiritual putrefaction."

Whatever *The Picture of Dorian Gray* owed directly to French Decadence and Huysmans in particular, Wilde made no secret of his large and enduring debt to France, his envy of the freer life of the artist there and his fascination with French exploration, in both art and behavior, into "illicit" regions of the self. "French by sympathy," he once said, "I am Irish by race and the English have condemned me to speak the language of Shakespeare." On his frequent trips to Paris he eagerly sought out artists and writers, meeting among others Hugo, Verlaine, Mallarmé, Zola, the Goncourts, Gide, and Pierre Louÿs, impressing some of them, baffling others, and disgusting quite a few. He had his hair curled in imitation of a bust of Nero he had seen in the Louvre, carried an ivory walking stick such as Balzac had affected, and wore a white dressing gown modeled on the monk's cowl that Balzac had worn at his writing desk. Indeed, he spoke of himself at times as a "character" out of Balzac.

In 1888, though, he wrote to William Henley that "Flaubert is my master, and when I get on with my translation of the *Tentation* [a project he never carried out] I shall be Flaubert II, *Roi par grâce de Dieu,* and I hope something else beyond." He also "adored" Baudelaire, and one of his biographers, Philippe Julian, tells us that "what he wanted above all was a fantastic art like that which he had discovered in Gustave Moreau's studio." But though these enthusiasms were genuine enough, and the influence of Huysmans in particular was deep and long-lasting, the suspicion is unavoidable that France served Wilde most profoundly as a place of tutelage for his personality, his subversive gestures, his carefully orchestrated histrionics. Above all, it served to confirm him in his complicated, divided, and ultimately disastrous ambitions toward being a "ruler," a shaper of consciousnesses and souls.

In any case, once "decadence" and "decadent" had passed into common usage in England, their French antecedents became gradually obscured, at least in ordinary speech and thought. The hatred of Wilde which had begun to build up as he rose to celebrity, and which broke out fully with the scandals of his trials and imprisonment, had no need to keep linking him directly with the French; the question of whether his "decadence" was borrowed or his own receded into the background. Still, the prosecutor at one of his trials managed to elicit the information that Wilde smoked gold-tipped cigarettes and burned incense in his house, an iconography of elegant vice that was certainly not of English provenance. The citation of these things seems to have made a strong impression on the xenophobic jurors.

By the time of Wilde's death in Paris in 1900 "decadence" had been firmly attached to his person and much of his work (*Dorian Gray, Lord Arthur Savile's Crime, Salomé,* and many of the earlier poems; the fairy tales remained a puzzling exception). It had also attached itself to a whole body of lesser contemporary artists and writers—and one possibly greater one, Aubrey Beardsley—and to the behavior of any number of acolytes and poseurs. To the virile, or as we might say "macho," British mind Wilde's homosexuality was synonymous with his aestheticism and both were encompassed in his decadence. Shortly before he enlisted in the army in 1914, Wilde's older son, Cyril, who had been a small boy at the time of the trials and had never seen his father after that, wrote to his brother Vyvyan a letter that sums up as well as any document we possess the gross confusion and violent misapprehension that surrounded the subject:

All these years my great incentive has been to wipe that stain away; to retrieve, if may be, by some action of mine, a name no longer honoured in the land. The more I thought of this, the more convinced I became that, first and foremost, I must be a *man*. There was to be no cry of decadent artist, of effeminate aesthete, of weak-kneed degenerate.

Not long after this, Cyril was killed in action at the age of twenty-nine.

In his book *Son of Oscar Wilde,* Vyvyan (Holland, the name he had been given after the scandal) took a different, if just as confused and painfully naïve tack toward the question of Wilde's "decadence":

Many of his biographers have pointed to his admiration of human beauty, and particularly of male human beauty, as an indication of . . . decadence. This is manifestly unfair. Youth in all its forms has always been an inspiration to the poet and artist, and my father was only following the lead of Ruskin and Pater, neither of whom could be accused of decadence in admiring beauty for its own sake.

That Oscar Wilde was "immoral" in certain respects, that he was perverse, false in some ways, is scarcely to be denied. That he was, ultimately, self-destructive is an evident truth. But that he was *decadent?* The question is more than one of language or appellations. We ought to begin with the indictment in order to understand what is involved.

In a rational perspective we know Wilde as half-scapegoat, half-suicide. We know him also as a moral and spiritual acrobat, a man who could deceive himself and others with great sweep and rhetorical flair, who could exaggerate to the point of culpable folly and who could, for all his sophistication and cold wit, be as sentimental as any shopgirl. "What wisdom is to the philosopher, what God is to his saint, you are to me," he once wrote to Alfred Douglas. There is something deeply unconvincing as well as pathetic about Wilde's investment of so much grand emotion in a youth who accepted it without reciprocating (although all the evidence suggests that Douglas was in no way malicious).

Once his fortunes fell he pitied himself without cease, after having previously pitied almost no one else. There can be few more sorrowful and at the same time more embarrassing documents in the social history of literature than a letter Wilde wrote to the Home Secretary in 1896 in which he pleaded for pardon or parole (neither of which was granted). "He was suffering," Wilde said of himself, "from the most horrible form of erotomania, which had made him forget his wife and children, his high social position in London and Paris, his European distinction as an artist . . . his very humanity itself, and left him the hopeless prey of the most revolting passions." That not long after his release the next year he resumed his homosexual life, his last years being marked by continual promiscuity with Italian peasant boys and young Parisian hustlers, is an indication not of his hypocrisy, and certainly not of his baseness, but of his confusion and divided self.

Well, what has all this to do with decadence? The word is not supple enough to contain his contradictions. The effect of applying it to him is to arrest him in a kind of paralysis or to impel him backward, exhibiting him as outside the central moral and psychic energies and currents of his time, a spectator and solipsist, when the truth was that he was at the active heart of the age.

He was, it has become clear, the organizer and leading performer of a drama distinguished by its peculiar fusion of conscious and unconscious motives and by its having been made to serve as the crystallization of a cultural epoch. A great florid, self-appreciating personality (or so it appeared), he arranged the world around himself and reigned briefly over its consciousness, paralyzing its resistance and beating back its detestation through dazzling, prestidigious acts; until he miscalculated and the great flamboyant, but also adventurous, life collapsed.

"I used to rely on my personality," he wrote to Robert Ross a year before his death. "Now I know that my personality really rested on the fiction of *position*. Having lost position, I find my personality of no avail." He might also have added that without position he found his ideas—those pioneering, risky, and so often liberating notions about art and life and the consciousness that plays between them—also of no avail. For the last few years of his life he seemed not to think; stricken, in exile, he awaited the resurrection of his thought in a future, forgiving world.

The miscalculation, the "error" pressing against a wall of hypocrisy and execration, fascinates us precisely by its association with the earlier triumphs and with the permanence of the ideas, and would have only a sleazy interest without those things. Had Wilde been merely a camp follower of the arts or a classic homosexual dandy for whom the elaborate and artful presentation of the self is the only interesting creation, he would exist now on the far borders of social and cultural history, a curio, an English counterpart of Count Robert de Montesquiou, Proust's Charlus, and not, as he unmistakably is, a deeply problematic ancestor.

Oscar Wilde, a monolith of the Yellow Nineties or, alternatively, the mauve decade: the reign of paradox; art for art's sake; sensibility stretching itself to a point of no return; prancing refinement; camp; decadence. This figure, who collided with the established, savagely proper public values of his time, moved toward the confrontation, rather, with a blind, absurd self-assurance: he sums up an era and a mode of fatality.

Still, it is all very strange. Wilde as an icon has outlasted the substantive basis of his fame or notoriety. Homosexuality, after all, scarcely strikes the sort of person who today would be interested in Wilde as the dizzying subversion of the natural order it was once so widely or at least publicly taken to be. To put oneself forward as an exponent and mannequin of the aesthetic way of life, tirelessly proclaiming its superiority to "practical," bourgeois styles, may seem to us old-fashioned or naïve but not pathological, certainly not malign.

Yet along with an air of lordly, ill-fated nonchalance, Wilde continues to give off an almost palpable impression of the contaminated, even the putrescent. The young Léon Daudet met him in Paris and wrote that "his voice was at once pallid and fat, words came tumbling out of his frightful slack mouth and when he would finish he would roar with laughter like a fat, satisfied, gossipy woman." Edmond de Goncourt described him as "an individual of doubtful sex who talks like a third-rate actor." "The great white slug" a sharp-tongued hostess of the period, Lady Colin Campbell, called him, and though there is fierce injustice in the description for those who knew and now know of his generosity and lack of malice, it secretly recommends itself to us anyway.

For whatever else he was, our need for clean, decisive dealings with history is satisfied by his availability as a cautionary figure and an epithet. Along with those familiar scenes of Roman debauchery (Fellini's *Satyricon* is the latest, most hyperbolic example) and images of Berlin in the twenties, which remain the prototypical expressions of what decadence is supposed to look like, the English nineties continue to provide us with our chief vulgarized sense of the word's historical incarnation. And Oscar Wilde, with his elegant corpulence, his languid wit and movements beyond the acceptable (he gave cigarette cases to some of his young male lovers, inscribed "for services rendered") is still the very figure of decadence as a supposed choice and style of life.

What we begin with, then, is his status as a representative. In his study of Wilde, Arthur Symons wrote that "if he might be supposed for a moment to represent anything but himself, he would be the perfect representation of all that is meant by the word 'decadence' as used in the nineties of the last century and the noughts of this." But of course he has not been allowed to represent only himself; in having been made to sum up a period, to serve as its identifying image and telltale ambassador to the future, Wilde has nearly disappeared in his own right, becoming emblematic, nominal, an abstraction.

He is to us one side of late Victorian sensibility and ethos, as Kipling or Henley might be said to be the opposing side. He is "decadence" or "aestheticism" as they are "imperialism." Abstractions. Impediments. Decadence is not a fact but a value judgment, a category of belief or opinion, and it is this insubstantial word that Wilde has carried out of his era, like an emissary bearing the key to a secret code, or more like Hester Prynne, on whose bosom the scarlet *A* was placed to indicate a palpability. But what really is adultery as a fact or an execration, and why should we need to personify it that way? And what does decadence mean in relation to Oscar Wilde, who was a man and not a condition?

In André Gide's *Journals* there is an odd sort of speculation about Wilde's movement between the type of consciousness that produces "objective" works of art or intellect and that which intuits its own nature as subject and problem and expends much of its energy wrestling with the dilemmas of self. "I believe," Gide writes, "that this affected aestheticism was for him merely an ingenious cloak to hide, while half-revealing, what he could not let be seen openly; to excuse, provide a text, and even apparently motivate, but that very motivation is a pretense. Here, as almost always, and often without the artist's even knowing it, it is the secret of the depths of the flesh that prompts, inspires and decides."

The "secret of the flesh" immediately brings to mind Wilde's homosexuality, and there is no doubt that Gide intends this. Yet the very vocabulary in which he couches his analysis, a diction of muted lyricism and metaphysical suggestion, indicates that it is not his real concern. He is not so much trying to explain Wilde as to place him, and especially to bring him under the protection of that unique dispensation by which the artist is, or has been, permitted a discrepancy between behavior and inner truth which in the rest of us would incur the charge of bad faith. Most significant, he attributes to his friend an ingeniousness which suggests that Wilde was in some command of his fate, that his actions, especially his dandyism and aesthetic poses, formed a strategy for survival. And Gide wrote elsewhere of Wilde's "strangely conscious" life, "in which even the fortuitous seemed deliberate."

Without having known Wilde, Hugo von Hoffmansthal drew a much darker meaning from the same evidence: "His aestheticism had something hysterical about it. All the jewels among which he pretended to live so voluptuously were like eyes petrified in death by the threat directed against him by life. Ceaselessly he challenged life and insulted reality, but he felt that life was lying in wait for him in the shadows, always ready to pounce."

Yet Bernard Shaw, who knew him, offers a very different opinion: "Oscar Wilde was no tragedian. He was the superb comedian of his century, one to whom misfortune, disgrace, imprisonment were external . . . His gaiety of soul was invulnerable." And Jorge Luis Borges, speculating from afar, wrote that "he was a man who despite being used to evil and misfortune retained an invulnerable innocence."

High-spirited and terrified, calculating and hysterical, invulnerable and full of torment—these ascriptions by fellow writers make up the poles between which Wilde's actuality must be sought. One's impression from all the evidence, especially his letters, is that the negative terms in these judgments describe him more nearly. Had Shaw, for example, known Wilde during the years after he was released from prison, or had he even known him well before that, he might have seen a being who was vulnerable to an extreme degree, whose gaiety was often forced and what we might call "tactical." In any case, confusion reigns about him now and did then, so that it was inevitable that he would be wrongly seen in his time. The confusion centered then, as in the popular mind it still does, on his life in relation to his work, his behavior in relation to his thought.

For those he alarmed, his "decadence" was to be discovered

in everything: the writings, the social attitudes, the physical appearance and gestures, the final disgrace. We have sorted that out now; if he was indeed decadent, the evidence does not lie in the writings, which except for some derivative and wholly sentimental early poems are at worst somewhat florid and labored and at best, as in the plays and fairy tales, brilliant and original. Above all, in the best of his imaginative writings and in essays like *The Soul of Man Under Socialism* and *The Decay of Lying,* he was the very opposite of anything "decadence" could mean; he moved forward, extended boundaries, helped clear away dead material to make room for the new.

"Do you know what the great drama is?" Gide reported Wilde as once saying to him. "It is that I have put my genius into my life and my talent into my work." But it was not nearly so simple. The relations between the two were intricate and embattled, more so than for the majority of important writers. There are times when Wilde's writing seems to have been tangential to his truest self, a means and not an end, a way to provide for himself still more occasions for celebrity, amazement, *effect.* He was not the first writer about whom this can be said, nor was he of course the last. Yet there is another sense in which his self, particularly his public one, was managed on behalf of the work, made to display itself in ways designed to protect the integrity, and even the life, of the writing. This is what Gide noticed and it throws much light on the question of Wilde's purported "decadence."

Lord Goring in *An Ideal Husband* is a character who in spirit closely resembles Wilde himself. The stage direction that "he is fond of being misunderstood . . . it gives him a post of vantage" is the sort of Wildean paradox or elegant reversal of accepted values that makes the plays the witty creations they are. At the same time it reveals the strategy Wilde adopted in order to cut through his time, to make it fall back, so to speak, and give him room.

In 1894, not long before his trials and imprisonment and when he was at the height of his fame and power, he revealed in more detail the motives and considerations of such a strategy. In a letter to a minor artist, Philip Houghton, he wrote that "to the world I seem, by intention on my part, a dilettante and dandy merely—it is not wise to show one's heart to the world—and as seriousness of manner is the disguise of the fool, folly in its exquisite modes of triviality and indifference and lack of care is the role of the wise man. In so vulnerable an age we all need masks."

"Do not wear your heart on your sleeve," Jean Cocteau, a master of such self-protective tactics, once told a young writer. In the aesthetic realm (which includes the provenance of work and its public fate) Wilde lied and practiced deception as almost all artists do, most obviously since art became cut off from public values and was frequently their adversary. If today this sort of scheming strikes some as less defensible, impairing, it seems, the "authenticity," the closeness to life that is wanted from artists now by many activists, in Wilde's time there would have been few to quarrel with it except for philistines (although there were more than enough of those). A comment he made on *Dorian Gray* offers an unrivaled justification for the process: "The supreme pleasure in literature is to realize the non-existent." Wilde is referring to what R. P. Blackmur called the artist's "incre-

[133]

ment" to Creation, an unreality by which we measure the real.

To protect this fragile unreality from the all too great pressures of the actual, from his era's moral biases and impermeable imagination, Wilde most likely felt himself forced in part to write the way he did: fairy tales that used a classic, "neutral" form to contain ardent contemporary perceptions; plays beneath whose surfaces of witty social observation existed a world of obliquely sensed absurdity and demented logic. It has not yet been widely noticed how so much of the dialogue in *The Importance of Being Earnest,* for example, resembles the disconnectedness and pointed illogic of Ionesco's early plays. In *Dorian Gray* the ruse was somewhat different, to write with apparent realism about what were actually fabulous desires, legends of human craving for an impossible perversity and so for an impossible freedom. "That strange coloured book of mine," Wilde once described it. "Basil Hallward is what I think I am: Lord Henry what the world thinks me: Dorian what I would like to be . . . in other ages."

All begins with an impulse toward protective coloration, camouflage, on the part of an original mind faced with the contumely of implacable tradition. The age was vulgar; England, Wilde once wrote to Douglas, was a place "where the worship of beauty and the passion of love are considered infamous." To appear as a dandy and dilettante would then be a means of safeguarding from uncomprehending and therefore intolerant public view the immensely vulnerable seriousness of his worship and passion; he would set about to be taken in the *wrong way* by the age's sober, steadfast, literal consciousness. And his true, inimitable offering would be discovered by minds on the outskirts, released from or ungoverned by Victorian earnestness and idolatry of the useful and prosaic, just as *he* was free of those things.

And so it has come about, in part. We see what his artistic and intellectual strengths were and admire them; we understand the strategic "misunderstanding." If we also retain a physical sense of him as corrupt, tainted, "decadent," that is another misunderstanding which remains to be cleared up.

The personal and sexual behavior was marked for a long time by a deceptiveness similar to that which governed the work. For a time Wilde benefited from the ironic fact that the Victorians thought of dandies and swells as necessarily being big men with the ladies. Later, and no doubt partly as a defensive tactic, he interpreted, or rationalized, sexual love between males as "higher," a matter of pure beauty, the Greek consideration. Yet to the theory that Wilde's masks and ruses were all designed to cover up his homosexuality, the reply is that he neither practiced as a homosexual nor showed any carnal leanings toward men until long after his reputation as an aesthete and dandy had been established. Later the two became intertwined; to protect the artistic self and to safeguard the erotic one involved many of the same tactics. Later still, the reckless, defiant, and, from the most obvious perspective, self-destructive elements of his nature broke through and he became an undisguised, indecorous— considering the times—homosexual. The result was, of course, the fatality brought down upon him by the trials.

Yet the self-destructiveness was mixed with something we have to think of as positive, an impulse of strange valor, as it is now possible to see. In the winter of 1895, a few months before the disastrous clash with Douglas' father, the Marquis of Queensberry, Wilde was in Algiers, where he talked with Gide about his new, open life as a homosexual. "My friends beg me to be careful," Gide reports him as saying. "But how can I be careful? That would be a backward step. I must go on as far as possible. I cannot go much further. Something is bound to happen . . . something else."

Something else. The words are resonant and poignant. It would have been a backward step for Wilde to retreat into hiding or to put on again the old disguises. (After his conviction at the second trial there was an opportunity for him to escape to France, from where he could not have been extradited; he of course refused to flee, and so went to prison.) He had to "go on." This surely reveals a strain of heroism in him. Besieged, far from conscious of all his motives, with an underside of adolescent bravado no doubt, and an element of suicidal loss of control, he was heroic nevertheless. It was valor of an order resembling that which had operated in his lifelong struggle for recognition that "immorality" was a necessary subject for art and that art itself was a form of truth. Very differently from what he had planned, his life and his work came together in those fateful months, everything expressed now in a "truth" both shared.

In refusing to go backward, to retrogress into silence or camouflage, Wilde advanced into an arena of public opprobrium and anathema where the destruction of his career and the loss of his family, his position, and indeed his self-esteem was accomplished. But what was accomplished there, too, as it would turn out, was a cutting through of public hypocrisy and communal deceit, an accession of truthfulness, an opening to the light. In bringing this about, Wilde did not so much serve the cause of homosexuality—as it happened, the immediate consequences of his trials and imprisonment were catastrophic for English homosexuals—as that of the forward movement of civilization, if we define that as the constant widening of consciousness, or at least its perpetual fertile change.

If "decadence" means, as it has always broadly meant, a backward movement or sterile arrest, the mulling over and taking to the self materials and actions that have been surpassed or left behind by society, a dwelling on values that are thought infertile and a consequent refusal to "advance," then it is difficult to see in what sense the word can be applied to Wilde. If we think of his erotic practices as decadent, it is only because we have borrowed the usage from his own time, which in turn borrowed it, without comprehension, from abroad.

On the intellectual and artistic side he was ahead of his era; his works make up the very opposite of what "decadence" is supposed to mean in relation to culture. They pointed toward the future, they carried an element of change. To see Wilde whole is to see an action and a condition—a life—that, whatever else was true, helped to destroy the rigid and complacent, helped to break up the frozen moral world. To think of him as "decadent" would be to abet the conspiracy through which our icy, unyielding moral terminology maintains its power to *settle* things, to bring complexity to heel.

In a letter to a friend after his release from prison, Wilde made a remark that indicates his own ultimate awareness of his besieged and mysterious condition. "I was a problem," he said, "for which there was no solution." The melancholy yet sage observation leaves us, or ought to, with a knowledge of the limits of speculation. It is a rebuke to our appetite for knowing, where knowledge is a form of illicit control, a means of denying fatality. To think, then, of Wilde as decadent would not be to isolate the problem but to offer the solution: such epithets paper over the holes in our existence while claiming to fill them in.

Apart from Wilde and Beardsley, the Decadent/Aesthetic period in England had little effect on the subsequent course of her art and literature. It is easy to forget that the nineties were dominated by writers like Shaw, James, Wells, Belloc, Kipling, Housman, and Francis Thompson, all entirely uncongenial in both temperament and style to the aesthetes and decadents. Of the latter, poets like Ernest Dowson and Theodore Wratislaw were rightly considered to be very minor figures and their work mostly derivative and insubstantial.

This verse was in fact the object of much ridicule, as were the affectations of "decadent" poseurs and camp followers. Richard Le Gallienne wrote a number of mocking poems on the subject, including the well-known "Décadent to His Soul," with the accent over the *e* naturally intended to point to the French origins. In the straightforward (and jingoistic) vein of "To the Reader" he lamented these alien influences and asked about the possibility of "hear[ing] an English song again." Lionel Thompson wrote in *The Cultured Fawn* in 1891 that "the point" today was "exquisite appreciation of pain, exquisite thrills of anguish, exquisite adoration of suffering." And Andrew Lang, the fairy-tale man, wrote with a certain justification in 1900 that "by picking holes in his boots, crushing in his hat and avoiding soap, any young man may achieve a comfortable degree of sordidness, and then, if his verses are immaterial, and his life suicidal, he may regard himself as Decadent indeed."

These critics had an easy target. Any serious development in art or thought, especially one with a subversive stance toward tradition, will always give rise to frivolity at its borders or to a seriousness without talent, which also amounts to frivolity. But such cultural insincerity, like any fashion, is transient. The future sorts things out. In a book on the nineties called *The Beardsley Period,* Osbert Burdette attempted a few years ago to distinguish what in the period was decadent, in the pejorative sense, from what was not, was vital and endured.

Beardsley, he wrote (and he might also have been describing Wilde), "accomplished in art the final overthrow of the complacency that had blinded Victorian eyes to the spiritual atrophy beneath the riches that it [*sic*] was accumulating. He showed the soul corrupting beneath the mask of industrial civilization." The just observation is reminiscent of a remark by Paul Tillich about moralism in art: "They call decay what is actually the creative expression of decay." At its best, in Beardsley and Wilde, decadence, in so far as it was used as a descriptive term, meant health.

But Burdette was still a victim of the word's perversion. "The decadence with which the century closed," he writes, "a decadence that affected, but neither explains nor created, the genius that chanced to flower on it . . . [this] decadence was an accident of the time; the genius was above it, but genius has no power over the moment of its birth." "It becomes extraordinary," he goes on, "that the Beardsley period should have been attacked more vehemently than the period against which it was reacting. The perversity and corruption are upon the earlier side and, compared with it, the Beardsley period is natural and healthy."

Burdette is right in this judgment, but there is something confused and inadequate about his larger argument. Because he accepts the designation without questioning its origins and its status as an epithet and a piece of jargon, he can only rescue "genius" from the grasp of "decadence" by calling the latter an accident. But this is only to say that genius is permanent or necessary, and the argument is necessarily *ex post facto*. At the time it was precisely Beardsley's and Wilde's purported decadence that made so many people blind to their genius or was used to deny it. And the truth was that "decadence" had almost no substantive meaning in England at this time, only a thin topical suggestiveness. The genius didn't flower in spite of the decadence or "above" it. There was no decadence but merely a word for what was not understood, and actions taken, gestures made, in the space that the word concealed.

5

IN 1948 THE BRITISH PHILOSOPHER C. E. M. JOAD published a detailed and painstaking inquiry into what he thought of as the phenomenon of decadence. The book is by far the most thoroughgoing endeavor of its kind, ranging over or at least touching upon many disparate subjects and trying to bring them under a guiding intelligence. Yet for all Joad's labor—more than four hundred pages of exposition, example, and argument—his work is curiously unresonant and intellectually sterile, amounting to an obsessive turning over of a few central ideas, or biases, as one is tempted to call them. Still, Joad's *Decadence* is extremely useful, since in its pursuit of the subject it goes down nearly every blind alley into which the word has enticed so many minds.

Joad necessarily starts with the assumption that decadence is historically actual, that it exists and so is capable of being identified. After acknowledging how difficult the word is to define, he nevertheless proceeds to define it in much the same way as it most often has been; in doing so, he gives an entirely unwitting revelation of how even systematic thinkers, perhaps *especially* they, are led by this strange, problematic word into error and even folly.

He begins by positing a good, or norm, which he calls the "object" in the light of which he sees decadence as a kind of denial or betrayal. This norm is never satisfactorily defined or even described, but it appears to consist in a type of Natural Law with a component of transcendence, a supernatural dimension similar to those of orthodox religions, though lacking in any specific doctrines or dogmas. It contains within itself or is coterminous with (and may simply summarize) all the moral and spiritual values that various societies have accepted as having a "non-human" origin and have lived by throughout history. These values derive, Joad says, from a recognition of some primal value, or deity as it might be, to which every human being is always subject. These values, in so far as they are linked to the Object (as they must be), are themselves "objective," which is to say they are not dependent on individual judgment, on private decisions or interpretations, but exist as the fixed, communal recognition of the "good" and "valuable" in themselves.

Beyond this, and as a necessary truth, the Object is non-contingent, not tied to particular circumstances; one can be sure that Joad would have been as fiercely opposed as any orthodox churchman to a notion such as that of "situational ethics." The implication of this is that no human experience ought to be valued for its own sake but only as it serves or fulfills the Object, the overriding and justifying dimension of both moral and ontological reality. And decadence, Joad argues, is in its most central manifestation precisely the valuing of experiences for their own sake or, even more radical a malfeasance, it is the flattening out of all experience as equally valuable or not.

It is beyond the scope of this book to discuss all the philosophical, intellectual, and historical difficulties Joad gets into, but much of what he says about decadence, especially when he purports to have found concrete historical manifestations of it, is relevant to our purpose. His comments on art and literature, which make up a very large part of his inquiry, are most germane of all.

To begin with, as one might have predicted from his general premises and approach, he is a reactionary in artistic matters, of an especially naïve and foolish kind. This cast of mind exhibits itself throughout the course of the book but perhaps most flagrantly in the repeated and obtuse distinction Joad makes between "form" and "content," in which—as all our high-school art appreciation courses had it—content is what is being said and form is the manner of saying it.

"Form without content is often put forward as a definition or, at least, a sign of decadence," he writes in obvious agreement with the proposition. But how can one conceive of such a thing? Étienne Gilson once wrote that "form is that by virtue of which a thing is the very thing it is and not some other thing," a definition that ought to open our eyes to the indissolubility of the relationship and so make it impossible to perpetuate the silly dichotomy. But of course what Joad is saying, what is always implicit in such formulations, is that *new forms* are without content, which is to say content of a familiar, accepted, and, at the higher levels of artistic and intellectual work, sanctified kind. Since he cannot see any such substance in works with new and what he calls "bizarre" forms, Joad concludes that the form is being presented for its own sake instead of being, as he thinks it is supposed to be in art, at the service of one or another aspect of the Object.

The content or substance Joad wants to see in works of art is familiar, to be sure, but also, naturally, of a positive sort, a "healthy" sort. "I want my thoughts to be elevated and enlarged and my feelings to be stimulated and refined," he writes. The prime criterion for artistic work that will fulfill these comfortable, hygienic aspirations is "nature," which in Joad's system is more or less synonymous with the Object.

"The further pictorial art withdraws from nature, the less satisfactory are the results," he says, and so gives the show away.

For in Joad's scheme nature is not simply the ground and inspiration of imagination, an assumption that has been present throughout history (although there is also a perennial strain in art that sees nature as something to *oppose*). Nature exists, in his view, to be imitated, an idea whose historical career and present deficiencies need no recapitulation here. It follows that his standards for art works are wholly, adamantly traditional and realistic. "In the classical age," he writes, "there were certain agreed criteria of literary and artistic excellence. A good work possessed certain virtues, for example, lucidity, poise, balance, elegance, measure and harmony."

Now, the things to notice about this assertion are how the term "classical" acts to incorporate and jealously guard "good" and how the litany of virtues fits only a narrow sector of the historical life of art. Good art for Joad is moral art, and that in turn is art which maintains the virtues that were once briefly decided upon, the so-called classical, "natural" values. This is the prescription that has been used to attack every new departure in the arts throughout history, most vehemently of course in the past hundred years or so.

And so we are brought to "decadence." The decadent in art and literature (and by extension in every human area) is whatever rejects classical values and the fixed relation of the moral—more narrowly the ethical—to the aesthetic or to the philosophic and psychological as well. Because new forms necessarily reject some or all classic values and repudiate art's identity with ethical truth, all such forms in Joad's cosmology are decadent by definition. Since there is no "content" in innovative work, the form is seen as making up the whole. "The form and style of the work," he writes, "which, rightly regarded, are only the vehicles in which the artist or writer brings his wares to market to offer them to the public, become themselves the wares."

The absurdity of thinking of art as composed of ready-made materials and appropriate subjects, of the imagination as a kind of commercial packager and the artist as a push-cart vendor, is nowhere more evident than in Joad's estimates of particular arts and artists. "The absence of ornament in architecture and the corresponding insistence upon the performance of function is a sign of decadence," he writes. Debussy was decadent, he says, because as one listens to his music "vitality and zest for life drain away." Virginia Woolf was decadent because her books were preoccupied with "the minutiae of experience and trivialities of personal relationship" and because of "her persistent refusal to grade, to give moral marks or to assign values."

Such insistence on vitality, conceived of as a pumping up of the spirit, on largeness of view, and on the "grading" of human experience and behavior along a moral spectrum, is a perennial element in attacks on new art and defenses of the old. *Life* magazine used to run editorials calling for a "healthier" national literature and castigating most of our best writers for their "narrow" vision and "sordid" themes, without, however, thinking to call them decadent. But the word has a long history of employment in such contexts. As Renato Poggioli has written in *The Theory of the Avant-Garde,* "the most facile and frequent motif of hostile criticism is to accuse all avant-garde art of decadence."

Tolstoy's *What Is Art?* bristles with such accusations. "The Decadents and aesthetes of the type once represented by Oscar Wilde," he writes, "select as a theme for their productions the denial of morality and the laudation of vice." More interestingly, because it perfectly fuses the moralistic and the aesthetically insensitive (and as he grew old, Tolstoy's philistine strain grew more pronounced), he says of Baudelaire, whom he considered the father and dark angel of literary decadence, that "the feelings the poet transmits are evil and very base ones. And these feelings are always, and purposely, expressed by him with eccentricity and lack of clearness." And he goes on to grumble about the well-known lines of Verlaine, another of his decadent exemplars—"*la neige incertaine / Luit comme du sable*"—"how can snow shine like sand?" Behind Tolstoy's criticism of "decadent" writing lay his late-blooming belief in literature as progressive. "Art, like speech," he writes, "is a means of communication and therefore of progress, that is, of the movement of humanity forwards towards perfection."

Such moralism and didactic zeal as Tolstoy's and Joad's, or John Gardner's, in his recent heavy-handed book *On Moral Fiction,* is not essential, however, to the idea of literary and artistic decadence, an idea that has persisted in academic quarters as one means of organizing the chronology of the imagination. The belief that there are periods in the arts when, after a brilliant flowering, decline sets in and an ertswhile robustness lapses into debility and enervation goes on being held in the face of the clearest truth that powerful art does not "give way" to weak art, turning into it like an organism running down, although what we think of as strong art may indeed be succeeded by the weak. The idea would seem to derive from the same anthropomorphic bent, the same impulse to interpret from analogy to the body's fate, that we have seen at work in the political and social spheres.

That there have been and continue to be times of great artistic vigor and assured style followed by ones of depleted energy and uncertain manner, and that periods of imitation often succeed ones of notable originality, is scarcely to be denied. But the problem with thinking of those presumably inferior cultural eras as "decadent" begins with the historical fact that in art both the imitative and the crude—the seemingly bereft of skill—have been accorded the designation. And you cannot have it both ways: the imitative strives to be like the model; the crude or primitive represents precisely a failure to be like it, to reach its level.

Now, imitation in art may be bad (Ortega y Gasset called it "nothing," a principle of emptiness), but to call it decadent is to abandon the word's only plausible meaning. For if "decadence" means a "falling down" or "away," which is what Joad means by it and what it has always fundamentally meant in serious discourse, and which is what every dictionary offers as its root sense, then the imitative by its very nature could hardly be decadent, since its repetition of what has been validated and sanctified in the imaginative realm is proof of its respect for, its unquestioning acceptance of, the norm. One may argue that the imitative might be considered decadent because it falls away from an ideal of originality, but this is not how critics or academics, in their concern for safety in cultural judgments, have ever argued. In any case, imitation is its own condemnation and has no need for "decadence" to inform us about itself.

The reason for this academic tropism toward "decadence"

as a category is most likely that, consciously or not, historians of culture generally argue, as I have said, from the example of the body. And, consciously or not, they believe in progress, however they may qualify the idea by turning it, for instance, into a notion of cyclic rather than linear advance. In this view, imitation, the arrest of an art at some high level, its being made to spin around on itself, impedes the flow of progress and stops things in their tracks.

An even greater and more obvious blow to progress, its apparent reversal, is the advent of the crude and uncertain or of smaller creations in artistic life. What so upsets most historians of later Roman painting, to take one example, is the seeming loss of mastery in the depiction of the human body. What so displeased Joad about Debussy and Virginia Woolf, and displeases many critics of fiction today about their contemporaries, is the modest nature of their ambitions and their achievements in relation to those of the giants of nineteenth-century literature and music.

Yet if art becomes rougher or smaller, this is only in comparison to the finer or bigger, and matters only if one holds the latter qualities as ideals. In that case one would be judging works of art not in themselves but by reference to abstract measurements, which is of course how works of art have generally been judged by professional judges. But artists at any time may choose to be smaller or cruder than their predecessors, out of a wish, it may be, for a release from the grand, the confidently *finished*. Or else they may be like Paul Klee, who said that at the beginning of his career he had wanted to create an art "as solid and enduring as that of the museums" but had found himself in actuality able to proceed as a painter only through the inspiration—the examples of possibility—of things as tiny and transient as the forms of sea life he once observed through the glass bottom of a boat in the Bay of Naples. They may, that is, be *able* to do only lesser or cruder work as the price—if it is one—of refusing to imitate. In any case, the smaller or cruder is not necessarily the inferior and, beyond that, there is no logical or inevitable or inherent process by which the superior in art yields to the inferior, health to sickness, or monumentality to depletion.

In his introduction to Huysmans' *À Rebours,* Havelock Ellis wrote that "there seems to be no more pronounced mark of the decadence of a people and its literature than a servile and rigid subserviency to rule." This condition may be unfortunate but it has nothing to do with "decadence," if the word is to mean anything at all. With his wonderfully clear sense of how "decadence" has been corrupted as a word, Rémy de Gourmont asserted that in relation to art it can mean only imitation, in which case it would not mean what it always has formally. And he pointed out how in so volatile a linguistic atmosphere as that of late-nineteenth-century France, poets like Verlaine and Mallarmé found it possible to assimilate the idea of decadence as imitation to its exact opposite—the idea of innovation. Going even further to the root of the question, de Gourmont challenged the habit of "blaming" bad or inferior periods of art on a process of the degeneration of the superior:

From Racine to Vigny, France produced no great poet. It is a fact . . . But it is not necessary to go beyond the fact itself, nor to attribute to it an absurd character of logic and necessity. Poetry was asleep during the eighteenth century, through a lack of poets; but this failure was not the result of an excessively rich flowering of poets earlier. It was what it was and nothing more. If we give it the name of decadence, we admit a sort of mysterious organism—a being, a woman, Poetry, which is born, reproduces, and dies at almost regular intervals, in accordance with the habits of human generation—an agreeable conception, a subject for a dissertation or a lecture.

The dissertations continue to be written and the lectures given. In *Gates of Eden,* a frequently perceptive book on the intellectual life of the 1960s, Morris Dickstein speaks of the unsure experiments of contemporary American writers like John Barth, Donald Barthelme, and Thomas Pynchon as constituting the "decadence of Modernism." What is wrong with this formulation, to begin with, is the premise that there is in fact such a thing as Modernism, that it is a species of being, an entity. Against the conventional wisdom, I would suggest that it is actually only a label, a term whose origins are obscure but which has been given currency and status in the academy, where most such nomenclature—Expressionism, Post-Christian, and so on—generally flourishes. But of course the great literature of the earlier part of the century has to be regarded metaphorically as an organism, a creature, in order for it to be capable of decadence, capable, that is, of having a life-cycle of the kind de Gourmont spoke about.

Of what use is an ascription of "decadence" to the writing that has followed Proust, Joyce, Eliot, Mann, and the rest? If newer writing is inferior, this isn't because its predecessor had fallen into a sort of old age and decrepitude. The earlier writing was what it was; you may search for the grounds of its amplitude, which is what the subsequent writing is always measured against, and find them perhaps in any number of social or psychic conditions. But those aren't its *causes.* The newer writing is what it is, in itself, and in relation to the past, naturally, but not totally dependent on it. Influences abound, granted, learning takes place, models are accepted or rejected. But literature is not written to compose literary history; moreover, the past may be burdensome or even dictatorial, but it is never an absolute monarch.

Serious writers at any time write as they will and as they must. They don't "fall down" or "away from" standards, for the standards themselves are constantly changing and new writing is precisely what changes them. Only a lofty, categorizing, anthropomorphizing impulse, one whose effect, if not intention, is to turn art into the material for dissertations, would find decadence in what is really fluctuation, the long rhythms of human expression. In cultural matters at least, "decadence" explains nothing and reveals nothing but our apparently unappeasable hunger for neat, fateful explanations of the essentially mysterious processes of creation.

"What those who speak of a decadent society or a decadent person mean," Joad wrote, "must have something in common with what is meant when they speak of a decadent literature." There is some truth to this, though it is diminishing as the word splits more and more sharply into its academic and popular usages. What is common to all employment of "decadence" as a pejorative is a quality of accusation, to the point of anathema, in the interest of a defense of something valued, felt to be essential or, if it does not yet exist, deeply desired. This function of the word has frequently led to its being used to denote opposites at the same time. In the eighteenth century, for example, French churchmen thought the nation was growing decadent because of the waning of religious spirit and practice, while anti-clericals argued that her decadence was due precisely to the persistence of religious institutions.

Intellectual and cultural history is full of instances of "decadence" being used as a club to beat what is seen as the betrayal or repudiation of one or another value. Oswald Spengler thought the "giganticism" and inflation of the American mind and imagination absolute proofs of our decadence, and wrote, in defense presumably of an ideal of discretion or elitism, that "nothing more clearly displays the decadence of Western art since the middle of the nineteenth century than its absurd mass-wide rendering of nudes." According to Konrad Swart, Charles Péguy thought the "degeneration of republican idealism into a despicable republican practice . . . perfectly illustrated how decadence ensued from the replacement of a mystique by a politique."

In Chekhov's *The Seagull,* Madame Arkadina calls her son "decadent" after watching the abortive play he has written in part as an attack on her own brand of conventional, "decadent" theater. Besides condemning as decadent all erotic subjects in literature, the aged Tolstoy asserted that the "shutting out of the masses from the pleasures of art" was a central characteristic of a decadent culture. Even Oscar Wilde, the unrivaled victim of the word's vagueness and malleability, contributed to the confusion. In *The Decay of Lying* his spokesman Vivian says that "the third stage is when life gets the upper hand and drives Art out into the wilderness. This is the true decadence and it is from this that we are now suffering." Here the primacy of art is being defended against the "decadence" of all that refuses to acknowledge it.

Although he never wrote a sustained work on the subject, Nietzsche's writings are full of comments on and references to decadence, and these hundreds of occasions make up a lexicon of the word's uses as a term of disapprobation, as well as of everything about it that is generally ambiguous and disconcerting. At the center of his obsession with the decadent is his conviction that civilization went wrong at a very early date. In *The Will to Power,* the book of his which uses the word most vehemently and in the most diverse and startling contexts, he writes that "the great Greek philosophers represent the decadence of every Greek excellence and make it contagious."

His argument, which will recommend itself only to those who share his fundamental interpretations of human experience in history, was that philosophy had the effect of making virtue "abstract," which in turn was "the greatest temptation to make oneself abstract: i.e., to detach oneself." Writing about Socrates, he says that "one had only one choice: either to perish or to be absurdly rational." He means that the disintegration of the age, caused by what he interprets as the excessive demands of the instincts, could be cured only by a Socratic type of rational control. But this control was decadent because it set itself up against the instinctual life; it represented a decline, a "falling away."

Whether or not one accepts this theory of the relationship between rationality and the instinctive life, it is undeniable that Nietzsche's ascription of decadence to the birth of philosophic thinking runs counter to any use we could have imagined for the word. But Nietzsche is prodigal with such shifts or reversals of the word's previously accepted meanings and usages. Philosophy, religion, and morality (any moral system at all) are decadent or symptoms of decadence, he argues. "Woman has always conspired with the types of decadence, the priests, against the powerful, the strong, the men," because she "brings the children to the cult of piety, pity, love." "Ugliness signifies the decadence of a type"; "to let oneself be determined by one's environment is decadent"; *Don Quixote* is "part of the decadence of Spanish culture"; "the 'good' and 'bad' man are merely two types of decadent"; "one wonders whether a tendency towards generalizations is not already a symptom of decadence."

Though these formulations are intelligible and persuasive in varying degrees, the important thing about them is that they all arise from Nietzsche's violent decisions about what constitutes health or illness, vigor or debility, in individuals as well as in societies. Thought weakens the emotions; pity weakens the strong; generalizations take the edge off the specificities of the world; *Don Quixote* mocks the boldness of the chivalric imagination; "good" and "bad" participate in a system of moral evaluation that attenuates fierce, original human energy.

All this may be true, if such matters can ever be said to be true or false, but, in any case, Nietzsche's use of "decadent" to describe nearly every manifestation of what he sees as humanity's mistaken course leaves the word emptied of nearly all substance. After treatment like this it exists without specificity, as an expostulation, a black mark, a debit sign, its original stock of meaning, however unclear and contradictory that might have been, long since exhausted. De Gourmont might have been thinking of Nietzsche when he wrote that "stripped of its mysticism, its necessity, of all its historical genealogy, the idea of 'decadence' is reduced to a purely negative idea, to the simple idea of absence."

To begin to account for the passing of "decadence" through so many uses, so many oscillations, divergencies and reversals of meaning, its being, in different periods, both a curse and an aggressive term of honor (as it was in late-nineteenth-century France)—and its falling so easily into the simulacra of meaning that intellectual fashion of the kind we are witnessing today has the power to contrive—we have to see it as damaged, or vulnerable, from the start. To speak in this way of an "injured" word may seem an indulgence in the sort of anthropomorphism we have been rejecting. If this is so, one may describe it as a form of intellectual judo, using an opponent's strength or weight against him, or else as a species of homeotherapy.

Once again, there are few things more difficult intellectually than to trace the biography or career of a word, an abstraction concerning whose existence there are no *facts,* only instances of its appearance in the guise of facts. To get finally at "decadence," we must now appeal to a faculty or operation of the mind we can acknowledge in other less problematic areas. This movement is one that gives us a sensation of being in a sort of shady and embarrassing transaction with language, an irresolute and often enervating intercourse with it.

If "decadence" is anything it is an epithet, and epithets of an aggressive and not merely a descriptive kind, invective, all types of verbal blows against actualities, disguise a loss of power and give off a simultaneous feeling of wishfulness and fear. Words that seek to maim, to diminish or do away with parts of reality (or for that matter to enhance, enlarge, or transfigure them), issue from a realm of the mind in which magic still holds sway. Sticks and stones may break my bones, but an epithet will, through sorcery, turn them into powder.

Alberto Moravia has written shrewdly about the way epithets, ascriptions, and the like have functioned in the largest historical contexts:

During the Middle Ages, antiquity was completely alien to men because it was pagan, whereas the Middle Ages were Christian, and Christianity wanted to be, and was, the paradox and opposite of paganism. Christianity wanted, consciously wanted, antiquity to be alien and unknown, to be denied, ignored, thrust into obscurity. In order to achieve this result it performed a very simple operation: it gave sin and damnation the face of antiquity; or rather, it gave antiquity the face of sin and damnation.

Moravia might have added: Christianity gave antiquity the *name* of sin and damnation, it struck at the ancient world with epithets. "The later Roman poets were only decadent because the nineteenth century wanted them to be," a historian has written. Whatever is called decadent today receives the name as the result of a wish. For "decadence," the word, is an epithet, neither more nor less, and this should alert us at least to the possibility that there is nothing to which it actually and legitimately applies. A woman is not a "bitch," though we may call her one. Sexual offenders are not "fiends." Homosexuals are not "fruits" or "queers." The Chinese are not the "yellow peril."

"Decadence" is obviously not a noun of the order of "chair," but neither is it one of the order of "corruption," say, or "sadness," or even "perversion." As an adjective it has none of the types of existence of "refined" or "powerful" or "sensuous"; it offers only *reputed* physical data on which to base its claim to actuality. Its existence is purely negative. It is a word chosen to fill a space. It emerges as the underside or logical complement of something else, coerced into taking its place in our vocabularies by the pressure of something that needs an opposite, an enemy. "Decadence" is a scarecrow, a bogy, a red herring.

The "positive" reality of which "decadence" is the shadowy obverse or complement is composed (as Joad saw, while drawing the wrong implications) of all the standards and ideals by which societies have judged themselves and been judged, all the criteria and norms that have governed various aspects of public (and later private) existence, or that have been thought to govern them. These change throughout history, of course, but what has remained constant is the condition of mingled yearning and fear out of which something drastically and exemplarily "wrong" has been posited in order to buttress belief in, or at least adherence to, what is "right." Decadence has always been made to function as a presumed mode of behavior or action that stands as evidence of a withdrawal from normality; whether this results from weakness, ill will, bad faith, or cunning decision, it is always the outcome of a fatal principle. Centrally, and beyond moral categories, decadence has been thought of as a type of regression, a falling away from others in their advance toward the future.

It will be obvious that this function of decadence as a category strongly resembles that of evil or sin in religious structurings of the world. Decadence has, in fact, usually been regarded as a type of evil, a peculiar, limited, ingrowing face of the bad.

In Catholic doctrine, for example, evil is, theologically, the absence or deprivation of the good; decadence, to say it once again, is the absence of or departure from certain norms. Yet there is a crucial difference, which is that the idea of decadence is inseparably bound to one particular value or criterion to which religon, theoretically at least, has been hostile or indifferent. That value is "progress." In more serious modes of thinking, decadence has historically been seen as the end of a line of progress, a reversion following upon an arrest.

This idea of decadence as the opposite or obverse of progress is a source of much of the mythology, both vulgar and elegant, that surrounds the word and keeps it in being as fashionable description. If "progress" is itself the most undeterminable and undemonstrable of words when used outside the area of physically measurable actions, if it is an arbitrary reality, a category of wishful human judgment and not a "truth," then to be linked with it as its dark complement, its oppositional mode, as "decadence" is, means that the latter ought to be immediately suspect. But its very unreliability as an accurate descriptive makes it wonderfully available as an epithet. Together "progress" and "decadence" have moved through our language and our thought as poles between which lies a void.

If the ideas of progress and decadence are really two sides of an illusion, then their persistence is an illustration of the power of language and thought to keep the nonexistent in imaginary existence. We accept such unreality, the "lying" action of metaphor, for example, when it operates in its proper spheres: the creation of fictions in the aesthetic realm, one of whose purposes is to relieve us of the burden of the world's facticity, its givenness; or in scientific explorations, where it functions in connection with hypotheses. The metaphors of fiction and poetry, of all the arts for that matter, are in the service of what might have been and might be, and have the effect of giving us, through this added dimension of possibility, a space in which to exist *otherwise.* The question then is not whether or not such metaphors are true but whether they are real, whether in fact they create such a space. (In science the question is whether or not metaphors do lead to the discovery of actualities, real processes or conditions.)

This is what Picasso meant when he called art "the lie that leads to truth." But there is another type of lie or untruth in which existence isn't added to, in order to create a new truth, or provisionally reshaped, in order to expose its secrets, but, rather, is wrongly seen. Here history and the present are subjected to an action of metaphor whose effect is to destroy their actuality, in the mind at any rate. The metaphors of art and of science recognize the actualities of the world and go beyond them; those of illusion replace the actualities with themselves. Both "progress" and "decadence," the latter even more intractably, are metaphors that express both a wish that the world move one way or another and an assumption that it does.

In J. B. Bury's *The Idea of Progress* there is the following confident assertion: ". . . every great civilization of the past progressed to a point at which instead of advancing further it stood still and declined, to become the prey of younger societies or, if it survived, to stagnate. Arrest, decadence, stagnation has been the rule." In Oswald Spengler's immodest tome, *The Decline of the West,* the notion is repeated, this time with the addition of that familiar image drawn from human chronology: "Every culture passes through the age-phases of the individual man. Each has its childhood, youth, manhood and old age."

The trouble with such schemata, which have a recurring and apparently indestructible life in the mind, is that they are fictions of a particularly empty kind. As I have pointed out before, there is only the most dubious historical evidence that civilizations do grow old, stagnate, and die, and none at all for the belief that this occurs according to some iron law whose workings mirror the stages of an individual destiny. The Roman Empire did not grow old and die; it underwent assaults and transformations. The British Empire did not obey a principle of decadence; it lost strength and was finally dissolved through the operation of certain political and economic *facts,* none of which was inexorable.

What history appears to show, instead of a law of decadence, are the simultaneity of decline and advance ("There are no mere phenomena of decay; every decline is also a rise," R. W. Collingwood has written), and the potential convertibility of one form of human enterprise into another. The evidently powerful produces the secretly so; the appearance of weakness is discovered as actual strength, and the reverse; culture wanes in order to renew itself; empires "die" so that their parts may live; the immoral is the proof of the moral. There is an economy of the manifestations of human behavior and activity in the realm of values that might be compared to the principle of conservation of energy in the material world.

In the light of this, the notion of decadence in societies and cultures can be seen to be injurious to the integrity and wholeness of communal experience. If there is a "falling away" from a standard it can mean that the standard is outworn, lifeless, or an obstacle to growth, which has been true in every period of innovation—at bottom a movement of renewal—in the arts and other human realms. If a once-strong society has become weak or a once-flourishing culture infertile, what is the point of describing the new condition as "decadent," since it describes itself? To add "decadence" to descriptions of human history is to perform at best an act of supererogation, at worst one of radical misunderstanding.

So much for decadence as a perspective upon civilizations, cultures, and their fates. What remains to be said is something about the word in relation to the activities of particular human beings, its chief currency now.

The peculiar power of fashion is to coerce us into doing what we would not otherwise have done or thought of doing. Fashion arrives like a wind from nowhere. The world of appearances or behavior recommends itself differently, new compulsions make themselves known, old habits are deprived of status. Once a fashion is under way, there is an irony behind its reign in every sphere, an irony of which we are unconscious except in hindsight: the imitative, the derivative appears as the original.

For the adamantly, the professionally fashionable, the "pace-setters," new style seems an increment, something added to nature or creation, although its roots can always be found in another fashion, one that has been repudiated; fashions exist to undo one another. For the rest of us, fashions always bring a disturbing emptiness, an absence of authentic choice (to be resolutely unfashionable is also to feel coerced); a gap is present between being and gesture. If we submit, we find ourselves carried along, acting in such and such a way or wearing such and such a garment because it is being done or worn; if we hold out, we find ourselves off balance nevertheless, somehow jostled out of the way by time.

Caught up in a fashion, you experience an inability to determine—should you make the attempt—its true relation to yourself, since fashion is, by definition, what has been set in motion and maintained by *others,* what is meant by others. Fashion is also by definition the ephemeral masquerading as the permanent, the arbitrary as the inevitable. Fashion chooses rather than is chosen and imposes "truth" instead of allowing it to be determined.

All this is most evident in physical matters, in dress, decor, styles, in objects of various kinds—Tiffany lamps, Swedish modern, warm-up suits. When it comes to impalpable realities such as ideas or speech, the matter, naturally enough, becomes murky and complicated. Yet we all recognize that there are fashions in thought and expression that are every bit as imperious as those that rule in successive waves in the material world; there are temporary reigns of genres of consciousness, unstable but momentarily despotic systems of evaluation or interpretation (there can even be a fashion of opposition to evaluation or interpretation). Freudianism in its debased form (but, of course, all fashions of an intellectual kind are a debasement) has been a notable and flagrant example; Structuralism, or the Death of God, or the notion of Camp have been more subtle ones.

"Decadence" as a fashionable term is one of the subtlest and most elusive examples of all. Unlike Freudianism, or any body of thought or way of perception or interpretation that has a provenance in *somebody's* mind, but rather like Camp, whose status as a fashionable word has been a matter of assumptions and ascriptions that seemed to have emerged as the result of a conspiracy with no one at its head, "decadence," as a word, a diagnosis, or, as has been prominent lately, a perverse honorific, has simply been found to be there, on every fashionable tongue, in every fashionable typewriter. And this is so despite the fact that nobody seems to know what decadence truly is, although vulgar and superficial theories of it abound and many phenomena are put forward as instances of its presence among us.

Yet such is the tyranny of fashion that we are all presumed to know perfectly well what is meant by the word in its current uses, all of us, that is, who are supposed to know what anything means. We are presumed to know that it denotes a fact or action or condition of the same order as a number of other aspects of human behavior at the fringe; we are expected to be able to distinguish it from other such actualities, the way we distinguish anomie, say, or sexual perversion, or unorthodoxy of many other kinds.

One thing that makes this possible is that unlike even Camp, which appeared to be something quite new in human history (those who employ the word most casually are generally unaware of its material roots in Regency England and its verbal ones in France), decadence is accepted as a recurring and universal phenomenon; we are simply in a new phase or phases of what has always been known, always bound sooner or later to display itself. This gives the word an apparent solidity, a seeming facticity such as "human potential" or "Post-Christian" or the "new eroticism" can only pretend to. Being presumably historical, proven, "decadence" seems therefore to be free of the element of wishfulness that so evidently characterizes the other terms offered here as examples of intellectual fashion.

But a wish is there, even if it is a great deal more subtle and better masked. What is wanted, in all but some extreme and improbably eccentric cases, is not really the thing itself, whatever that might be. One can legitimately yearn for the end of Christianity or for a bisexual revolution as the advent of the body as source of redoubled pleasure, but to crave decadence would rightly be regarded as a pose, would be thought of in fact as a sign of decadence itself, the posturing quality of which has come to be one of its prominently regarded features. When Kenneth Tynan chats about decadence as though it were a charming native dance or jet-setters hold parties with a theme of "decadence," the testimony is only to falseness, pose, the inauthentic.

The desire, it seems likely, is for decadence to *exist*, to be present in one form or another, so that we can identify it, or at least seem to, and so gain a measure of control or power through knowingness (a rather different matter from knowledge) over another perplexing aspect of the life of behavior and values; we want it to exist so that we can have an attitude toward it. And we want to have an attitude because such a stance implies superiority over fate; we become judges, we decide about the world.

The fashion consists, to begin with, of the assumption that "decadence" does exist; the word chosen to denote the thing is then employed as an approved instrument, a certified agency of meaning, on the basis of a sly consensus. Crucial to the success of this enterprise, this conspiracy to inject another unnecessary meaning into the world, is the blotting out of the word's history, which this book is an attempt to restore. If we knew what the word had experienced before we took it up, what vicissitudes and turns of fortune, what assaults and betrayals and what infections it had incurred, we would most likely drop it, as a tainted object. The truth is that we want the phenomenon of decadence to be historical, but not the word.

The process by which "decadence" passed from being a serious word in political and cultural thinking and discourse to the status of a chic term, has been obscure and discontinuous. I say "serious" because, however ambiguous the word always was and however unstable its connections to the world outside language, its general employment until quite recently retained a core of thoughtfulness; something had been intended by its use that mattered centrally to the quality of experience and to its interpretation. Those years toward the end of the last century in France, when the air was filled with the word "decadence" as both a cultural call to arms and a political execration, saw the peak of its strange, contradictory, but still vigorous and significant life. Even in England, where in the thinner intellectual and artistic atmosphere "decadence" drifted more and more toward the status of a pure epithet, it continued to touch on real issues, on questions of value.

After the turn of the century—the Dreyfus case and the death of Oscar Wilde in Paris in 1900 mark the end of an intellectual and moral epoch, as well as of a historical one—there were revivals of "decadence" in connection with artistic phenomena, or rather with the sociology of art and its politics. The word was used to describe the bohemianism of the so-called Children of the Sun in England during the twenties, and the arid monumentality of Fascist or Nazi architecture (the irony here being of course the ascription by the dictators of decadence to the modern art and architecture of the democracies). And it would continue to have a narrow use for scholars to describe purportedly retrograde periods in civilizations and cultures, and for ideologues on the Left to describe their bourgeois enemies.

But more and more, as the new century went on, "decadence" became the term whose connotations are most familiar to us now. It increasingly indicated aspects of behavior that were heavily sexual or unfolded at the intersection of the erotic and the self-displaying; the images it suggested were those of strapping men in drag, European royal exiles in Portugal, orgies in Park Avenue or Belgravia apartments. The milieu it created in the mind became increasingly compounded of ennui, effeteness, languorous or belligerent self-indulgence. It became a word that triggered erotic and quasi-sinful associations. And it became at last almost entirely vulgarized, unhistorical, rootless, and resistant to any kind of scrutiny.

Although it isn't possible to trace the movement with anything close to precision, we can say that the word's heavily sexual and appetitive connotations, along with its element of bourgeois-baiting—a trivialization of the position of the formal Decadents—arose from the excesses and inauthenticities of the Decadent Period in France and its paler counterpart in England. The process was one of a degradation of thought and speech, a corruption of ideas about the world—not necessarily true but *real* ones—into jargon concerning it, unexamined assumptions about it, notions plucked from the air.

Actions that had been essentially literary and ideological—Gautier's characterization of Baudelaire's poetry as decadent, by which he meant finely attuned to disintegration and therefore "modern"; the gathering of dissident writers and artists around the magazine *Le Décadent;* the cries of rightists in defense of order and tradition—gave way to flamboyant gestures; issues of culture and politics, to the eccentricities and egoisms of personalities. Huysmans was succeeded by Jean Lorraine, the so-called Petronius of the Decadence, in whose hands it became a principle of literary shock. The word's momentary core of passionate seriousness was overwhelmed by the hurly-burly and arbitrariness of fashion.

Literary characters such as Huysmans' Des Esseintes or Wilde's Dorian Gray and Salome became models for behavior or, more accurately, figures in a typology of possible behavior in an outrageous mode. Sexual unorthodoxies such as the lesbianism of Baudelaire's imagination, the hermaphroditism of Gautier's, and the androgyny of much serious and, later, not so serious *fin-de-siècle* writing passed into the popular mind as actualities summed up by a word, or rather suffused by it, made identical to it.

This fate of "decadence" makes up one of the most arresting instances of life following art; a generation now took its cue from what others had dreamed up. The "decadent" became synonymous with the perverted, the sexually morbid, or extreme, and with the cult of strange pleasures in general. And there was a peculiar freezing of the substance of the word in the immediate past; its long wayward history was forgotten and it seemed to have arisen as the description of what had been invented or had first come to light in the 1880s and '90s.

One irony of this was that whatever decadence in its behavioral sense had been in Paris, it was a highly circumscribed phenomenon. As Raymond Rudorff writes in *La Belle Époque:* "The books of the so-called 'decadents,' the novels of Huysmans, Rachilde, Barrès and Villiers de l'Isle-Adam, with their preoccupations with themes of sadism and sexual aberration, were read by a limited public but helped form a widespread picture of Paris as a sink of iniquity or a Mecca for the votary of erotic and forbidden pleasures." And Rudorff goes on to say that "the great erotic legend of fin-de-siècle Paris was partly fostered by those who had a commercial interest in its propagation."

To a later generation, decadence would seem to have been invented in the 1920s, specifically in Berlin. And once again the bases of the invention were rumor and what we would now call "hype." Christopher Isherwood writes in his autobiography, *Christopher and His Kind:* "Wasn't Berlin's famous 'decadence' largely a commercial 'line' which the Berliners had instinctively developed in their competition with Paris? Paris had long since cornered the straight-girl market, so what was left for Berlin to offer its visitors but a masquerade of perversions?" The French pressure went further; even the notorious Berlin cabarets were organized in almost every detail on French models.

The legend of Berlin in the twenties as a center of decadence, the *locus classicus* of a culture decomposing through indulgence and excess, is another of the historical myths we cannot seem to let go. In his account of life during the Weimar Republic, *Before the Deluge,* Otto Friedrich writes that "the decadent Eroticism of the film [*The Blue Angel*] seems to express so perfectly the mood of Berlin in the late 20s." It does nothing of the kind, for there was no such mood. Every reliable witness we have testifies to the superficiality of the so-called decadent elements in Berlin life and to the unprecedented atmosphere of intellectual and artistic energy in Berlin during the Weimar years. In *Weimar Culture,* Peter Gay writes of the "unparalleled mental alertness" that prevailed in the city, "the passionate general concentration upon cultural life."

As the decade went on, there were, of course, heavy blows to morale—inflation, assassinations, political turmoil culminating in the swift rise of nazism. But these things did not prevent Germany in the twenties from being the richest source of new art and thought in the world, and nearly to the moment of the Nazi takeover the work went on. Berlin was the heart of it. Willy Haas, an editor and film critic, came from Prague after the war and later wrote:

I loved the rapid, quick-witted reply of the Berlin woman above everything, the keen, clear reaction of the Berlin audience in the theater, in the cabaret, on the street and in the cafe, that taking-nothing-solemnly yet taking seriously of things, that lovely, dry, cool and yet not cold atmosphere, the indescribable dynamic, the love for work, the enterprise, the readiness to take hard blows—and go on living.

"Berlin tasted of the future," the writer Carl Zuckmayer said. And Count Harry Kessler, a shrewd observer of the period, wrote in his diary (published long after his death under the title *In the Twenties*) that the new architecture, of which Berlin was so prominent an exemplar, "has to be understood as a new way of living, a new assessment of what life is for and how it should be lived."

Architecture has always been a criterion of a culture's "health," one of the most visible of all. That it was being created in Berlin, and throughout Germany, with such vigor and daring is among the truths of the era that give the lie to the notion of German decadence. For, once again, if decadence is to mean anything, it has to signify arrest, stagnation. But it did not mean anything, or rather it meant what anyone wanted it to mean. In *Weimar: A Cultural History,* Walter Laqueur writes that "the opposition of the Nazis to jazz . . . was of long standing; they had always denounced it as the decadent outpourings of Negro *Untermenschen*." To the Nazis everything new in culture, except their own type of regression to barbarism, was decadent. The infamous Exhibition of Degenerate Art in Munich in 1937 might just as easily have been called a show of Decadent art, for that was the word Hitler was no doubt fumbling for when he spoke at the opening ceremonies of the "merciless . . . campaign" he would wage on behalf of his "healthy, unspoilt people" against this modern art that was "contrary to nature."

And so, against the evidence, on the basis of an extraordinarily narrow and circumscribed actuality—which testified at least as much to the freeing from sexual inhibitions that the period afforded as to its "illness" and moral decay—"decadence" became attached to Germany and Berlin and passed over into our own chatter. Beyond all of it lay the shadow of Rome as remote prototype, but Rome was scarcely to be imitated; what was available as material for a fashion was only the remembered, and distorted, past.

It is impossible to determine when it was that we first began to notice that "decadence" and "decadent" were occurring more and more frequently in conversation and the media. The words had never gone out of use, but for a time they had remained obscure and narrowly applied. Then, like all intellectual fashions, or material ones for that matter, this one seemed to accrete, to pass at some invisible point from a series of scattered occasions into a kind of weather. Confined, as they are likely to continue to be, to a rather circumscribed ambiance of sophistication and cultural opportunism, but very active there, the words operate with unflagging currency as indices of knowingness, counters in a game of being on top or ahead.

Their burgeoning use can be said to have begun perhaps seven or eight years ago, as if after a signal that the seventies needed a new, hot descriptive. An article in *Women's Wear Daily,* one of the chief sources of the debasement of many words, reported on a fashionable New York party that one social leader found wanting because "decadence goes over better in Europe." Another piece in *WWD* refers to a dress designer named Claude Lagerfeld as the "baron of decadence" on the strength of his "trench-coats," "décolletage," and "thigh-slits." An article in *New Times* on bisexuality is entitled "Decadence by Invitation Only," the author concluding that such decadence "is the most self-confident I've seen." Another journal said of E. M Forster's previously unpublished novel, *Maurice,* that it was "too decadent for its own time [but] is ideally tailored to ours."

Ironies bristle around this silly assertion. *Maurice* was about a homosexual relationship and Forster suppressed it in 1914 not because he thought the novel—or homosexuality—decadent but, among other reasons, because the time was still too close to the Wilde scandal, which had abruptly and brutally reversed a growing openness about sexual proclivities and, understandably, forced British homosexuals into hiding. And that Forster continued to suppress the novel during his lifetime was due to his sense of discretion or, perhaps, his fear, but in any case not to fretfulness about the decadence of the work.

It might have startled the glib magazine writer, for whom the book was *too* decadent for its time—as though a thing can be just decadent enough—to have learned that Forster considered the word to have been almost universally misused, regarding it in the same manner as those admirers of Huysmans who understood its use as a counter-term to a vocabulary of "progress," materialism, and social conformity. Speaking of Des Esseintes, Forster wrote: "Was [he] decadent? Yes, and thank God. Yes, here again was a human being who had time to feel and experiment with his feelings, to taste and smell and arrange books and fabricate flowers, and be selfish and himself."

Forster's encomium was no doubt strategic, a sly blow against moral hypocrisy and mass values, but it points up how in his time, at least, the word still wavered between contradictory meanings and intentions and, more important, still retained a memory of the only positive value it has ever historically possessed. Today the word has entered into its patrimony of full debasement; it has inherited all the loose ends of aberrant behavior and perverse sensual inclination that cannot be comfortably fitted into our diagnostic or evaluative categories. As an adjective it functions now like a coating, a sleek enameled skin applied to the "unhealthy" but not fully sinful; as a noun it exists as a disturbing substance with shifting, blobby outlines, like some animated and threatening gel from a science-fiction horror film, or else as something with disquieting allure—a transvestite of fine beauty, a cult of witchcraft—toward which one half-turns and about which it is wise to have a contemporary attitude.

In a particular type of journalistic mind "decadence" occupies a fluid position between behavior and the arts, sometimes being a fusion of the two, as in an entertainment like *Oh! Calcutta,* or an entertainer such as Bette Midler. The musical *Cabaret,* with its reminders of the German twenties, was a ripe object for the bestowal of "decadence" by shallow, unhistorical minds. A critic wrote in the *New York Review of Books:* "When I reviewed the play *Cabaret,* I rebuked Joel Grey, as the MC, for being too playful about his decadence . . . I was wrong. Some of that German decadence probably was playful . . . it also gave us the German expressionist film-makers and Kurt Weill and so much else . . ." History, language, meaning all disappear together under the chic stupidity.

A couple of years ago there appeared in the *Village Voice,* another journal in which the debasement of language may profitably be studied, a theater review by Julius Novick entitled "All in Favor of Decadence." Novick was writing about *Hotel for Criminals,* a play or theater piece by Richard Foreman and Stanley Silverman, all of whose collaborative work has been in an avant-garde genre of abstraction and anti-narrative. After praising the production's "wonderful stylishness, elegance and precision," Novick goes on to complain about its lack of "substance" and asks, "but is not the triumph of style over substance (that is, over the *lack* of substance) an infallible diagnostic of decadence?"

This is, of course, the proposition that Joad advanced and that has been advanced as a criticism of innovative art for generations. As such it adds nothing to this inquiry into "decadence," but some further remarks of Novick's surely do. "But how do we feel about decadence, anyhow?" he writes. "Personally, I think I'm against it; I know I don't prefer it; but I can respect it, grudgingly, if it is done as well as it is done in *Hotel for Criminals."* It. Done. To "do" decadence as though it were finger painting or a new Brazilian dance or some form of erotic calisthenics. To be *for* or *against* it, as though it were a bond issue on the ballot; to *respect* it or not to respect it, as though it were a political position or a theory of cultural influence. It is all so painfully naïve, so illiterate under the appearance of sophistication. And it is all so *received.*

More than anything else, it is this quality of being received, handed down, and accepted without skepticism or surprise and then existing as impregnable conventional wisdom that distinguishes the idea and uses of "decadence" today. The malady inflicts itself everywhere and is no respecter of position. An eminent novelist-reviewer writes in *The New Yorker* that Peter Handke "has learned lessons, seems spiritually

akin to those fin-de-siècle exquisites, those deliberately decadent self-flagellants in search of the divine, Huysmans and
Baron Corvo." This is received knowledge with a vengeance,
and it is, like all received knowledge, untrue, first as history,
and then as language, the meaning of words.

At the beginning of the seventies *New York* magazine published one of its special issues on the forthcoming "season."
An editorial note declared that there was a "new spirit of
decadence abroad in the land . . . a pall of decadence . . .
colored not mauve, as in that other famous decadent era, but
a diabolical black, cast upon a protested virginal-white, as our
fashion noter notes." The articles that followed maintained
this level of prose—sleek, knowing, foolish. But one in particular sums up and crystallizes everything about the word
in its descent into pure reflex and the profound irresponsibility of intellectual fashion.

The piece is by a writer on pop subjects who has himself
a pop sensibility, a cultural and social critic exquisitely tuned
to the *Zeitgeist,* and is entitled "The Rites of Fall: Driving
the Demons Out, Letting the Good Times In." "After Camp
and pop, rock and schlock, the twenties, thirties and forties,"
he begins, "you say—'What's left?' The answer is *decadence.*" "Is this the final trend, the last wave?" he goes on.
"Decadence means the bottom is a long way down. Come,
let's explore it."

The exploration consists in repeating, in the resonant tones
of a cicerone to the obvious, nearly every cliché and pop-
historical opinion one has ever heard about decadence. "A
decadent is a man who hates civilization while lusting after
its most extreme refinements," he writes, repeating a vulgar
notion of the nineties. "This fall you'll be seeing a lot of

decadent film action," he says. "Movies about those great contemporary protagonists, the pimp and the whore—or man as sadistic tyrant and woman as masochistic slave, a very appropriate theme for the age of women's lib." The youth culture is decadent, he argues, because it wants an impossible "escape from the modern world."

Tristan und Isolde "provided the whole foundation for the decadent movement in music," he asserts, offering no intimation of what that might be but indicating that he has at least read his Nietzsche. "Now all we need is a good show of decadent painting—Gustave Moreau and Odilon Redon," he chuckles. Moreau—who accepted the word as an anti-bourgeois emblem but saw through it as an epithet: "there is a moment," he wrote, "when an art begins to take on the characteristics of other arts . . . at such moments shallow minds begin to speak of 'decadence.'" And Redon—who played no part whatever in the formal Decadent movement and whose work bears no conceivable relation to anything the word is supposed to describe or has ever described.

Perhaps most revealing of the absolute confusion that surrounds the word in our period is the writer's use of it to denote at one time a substance and at another a manner or style. He speaks of certain movies, for example, as being decadent because of their subjects or characters—pimps and prostitutes, and so on—yet at the same time refers to "decadent film action" as though the moviemaking itself possessed the quality. He calls *Death in Venice* a "nostalgic and decadent" film, and one is left wondering where he thinks the malady, or, more likely, the cachet, lies—in the subject or the style.

But for such a mind, operating with the counters of fashionable talk, toying with issues that were once taken seriously, a mind slick, plausible, and empty, it doesn't really matter. The question is one of sensation, effects, *frissons*. The word will serve; it can combat boredom, jazz up the atmosphere, make itself felt as a coloration (mauve? orange?), display itself as a verbal skyrocket. What is precision or even simple rough accuracy in the face of such vivaciousness? At one point the author informs his readers that "The Forsyte Saga" will be "repeated this fall in one decadent 24-hour marathon showing"—a stretch of time being made to carry on its back this adjective, this free-lance epithet. The degradation of a piece of language can hardly be taken much further.

There are many more recent episodes in the career of "decadence" that could be cited, for the shabby exploitation of its vagueness shows no sign of letting up. But this seems a good place to end our inquiry. Fashions come and go, and it may be that the idea of decadence will suffer the same fate as so many other glib assumptions about the nature of reality. For that surely is what is at stake. "Decadence . . . a word for the lazy . . . for ignorant pedagogues," to call up Baudelaire's anathema once again. And he went on to say that it was a word behind which we shelter our "lack of curiosity regarding the Law." This is a mysterious remark. What Law is the poet referring to? Perhaps what Baudelaire meant is at the very core of what is alarming about our complacency in the face of the degradation of language.

The Law. We impose between ourselves and the deepest actuality of things a screen of indifference behind which is dismay. The Law is what is, what truly exists and happens, what cannot be reduced to our opinions, our "slants." Certain fashions in behavior create screens by which are blocked out the ravages of the ego, which is then converted into a series of statements or attitudes. Pedagogy is the practice of creating screens to mask the Law from our sight in formal ways, through language, through terminology. And "decadence" supports this evasion, this mode of laziness, by being a label, not the sign of a fact, not an insight. As such it is representative, and that is what has summoned up such passion as I may have displayed in these pages. No single word alone could justify this effort, but what might do so is a class of words, revelatory of some of the ways we cheat ourselves of truth through language.

In a recent book, *Art Against Ideology*, Ernst Fischer asks: "Should not the concept of decadence, so often misinterpreted and misused, be abandoned altogether?" It is Renan's old wish: to banish this injured and vacant word from history. But no one is empowered to effect the exile. The word will go on recommending itself to the shallow, the thoughtless and imitative, the academically frozen: monkey-minds. And the words for all the qualities that "decadence" is supposed to connote—"self-indulgence," "effeteness," "depravity," "brittle sensuality," "hedonism," and the rest—will have their own, already so difficult, task made harder still. The work of identifying the most fluid and opaque aspects of our behavior—a task that is synonymous with culture itself—will continue to be complicated and undone by the intrusion of this catch-all, this portmanteau stuffed with emptiness.